GRAVITY

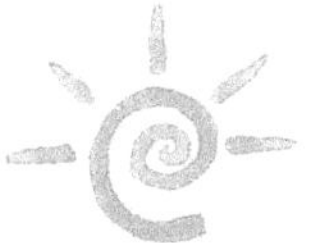

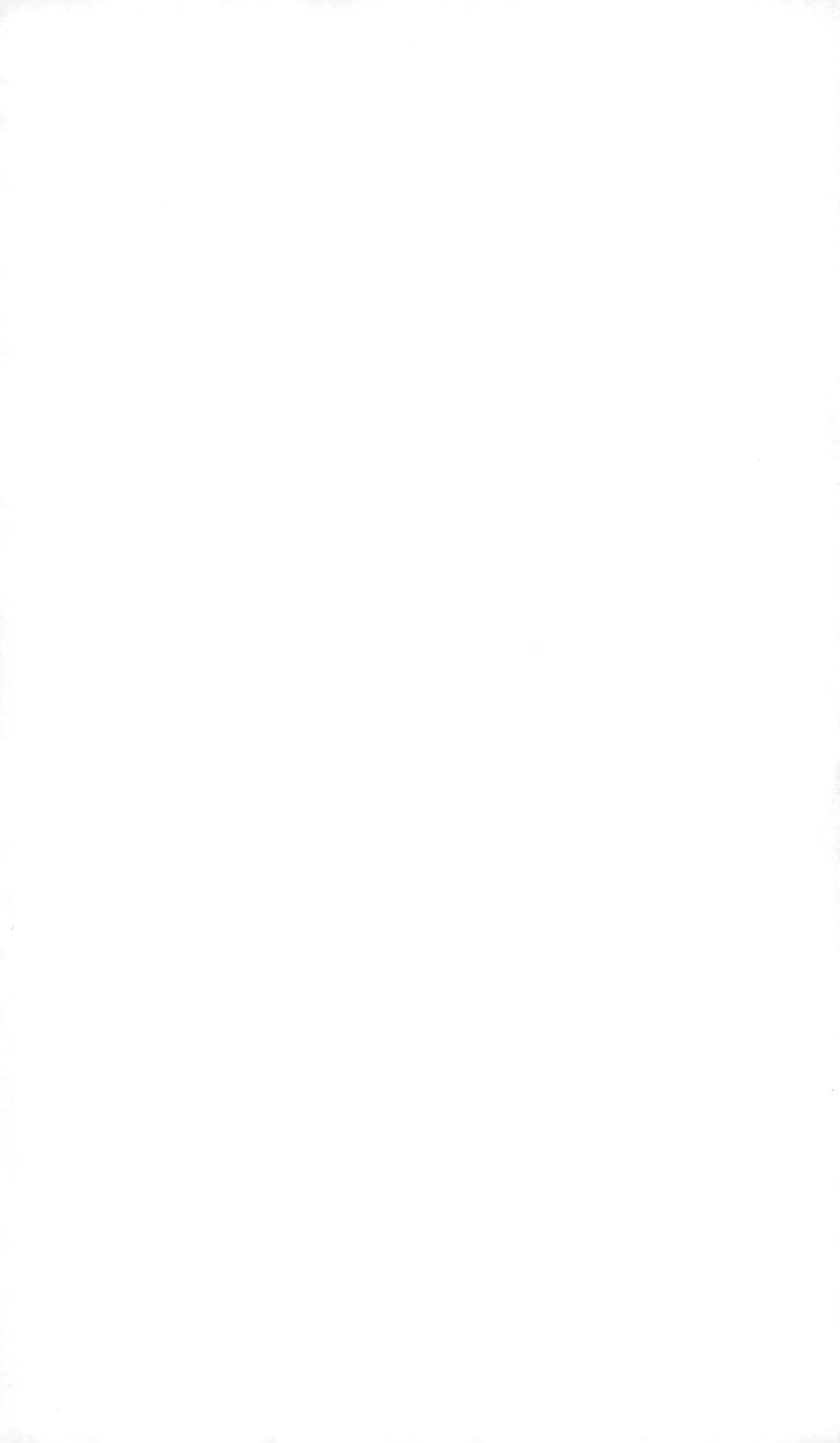

GRAVITY

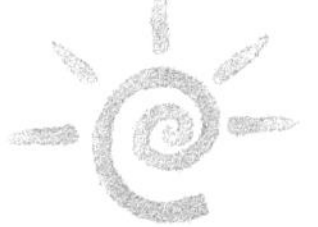

poetry and images

II

Chuck Alen

GRAVITY

poetry and images

II

ISBN: 979-8-9937366-1-7 (Paperback Edition)

Cover/Illustrations: Chuck Alen

Published by Waking Tree
www.wakingtree.com

For Mom
1944-2025

Contents

Introduction

Be it the magical force that keeps our feet on the ground or the constant draw between us as individuals, we see the impacts of gravity every day.

This simple word represents that which pulls on every level of our existence. It is a descriptor of what ultimately drives us towards both the dark and the light. It can be used to relate how we are compelled together by ephemeral community in this experiment of human existence or pulled apart by individual fears that drive wedges in between.

From the galaxies, planets, and stars to the subatomic realm, gravity references inter-actions operating at both the intangibly grand and the impossibly small scale.

Given that these interactions can be so ubiquitous, we often fool ourselves into thinking that they are insignificant. This would be a short-sighted mistake likely leading to a lack of comprehension of the fact that everything we are is seemingly born out of these various interplays. One could even be so bold as to say that we may be nothing more than an indirect expression of these interactions.

All of this may lead you to ponder ..Are we all just part of a puzzle trying to put itself back together or perhaps a shattered glass still figuring out a way to become the vessel it once was?

...but who really knows.

This book explores the varied interpretations of "Gravity" through poems and accompanying artwork. From physics to emotion, each section represents a different way we can understand this expression of attraction.

The Gravity of...... **Spirit**

The Gravity of...... **Space**

The Gravity of...... **Fear**

The Gravity of...... **Earth**

The Gravity of...... **Love**

SPIRIT

We dance in the miracle
of being lost to the winds of
our minds
our hearts bring us to the truth
of our being

we are never alone and never
have been
we can feel alone
but that is only the call of a
false prophet

gravity of spirit

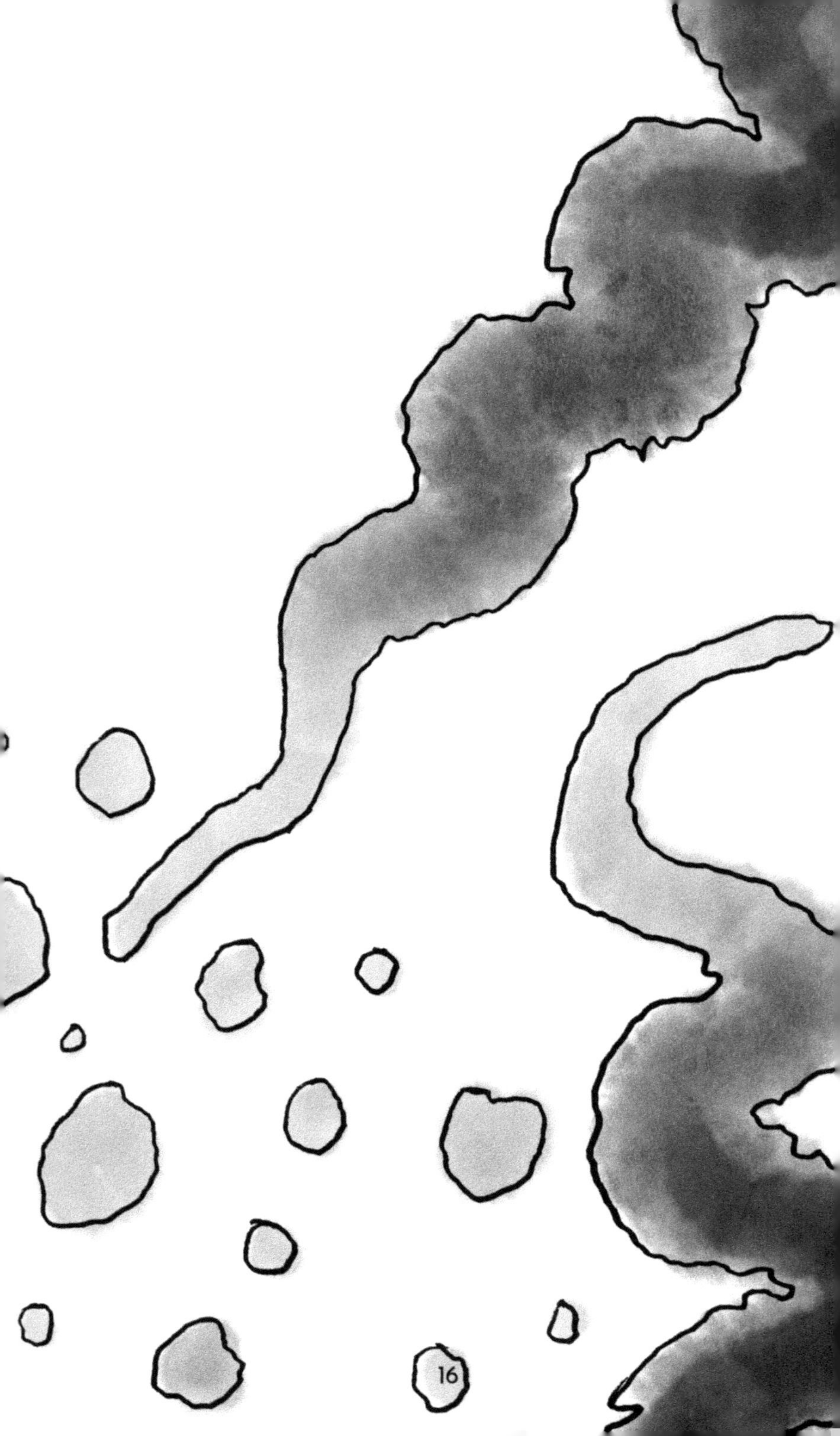

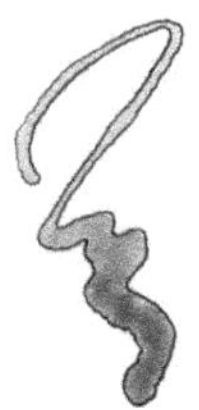

just as one is born
one dies and returns to be
a part of it all

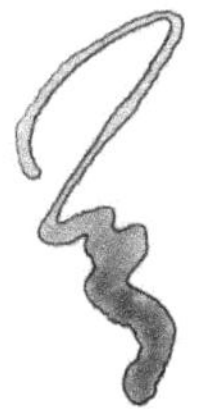

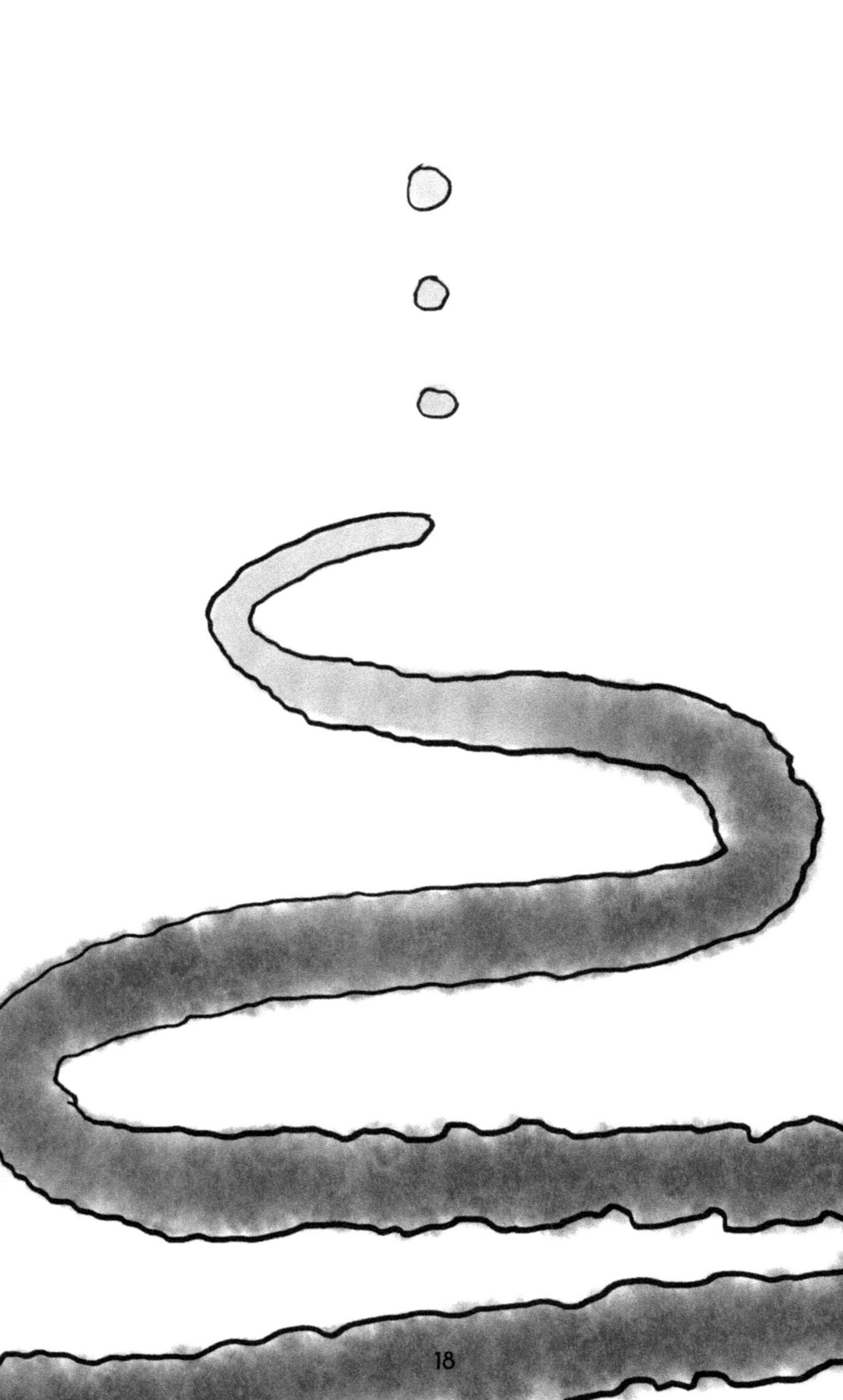

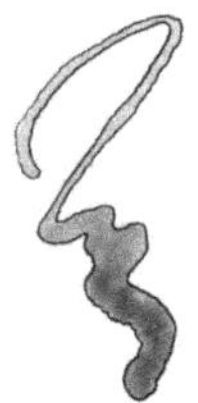

the lonely soul seeks
a path to congregation
communally drawn

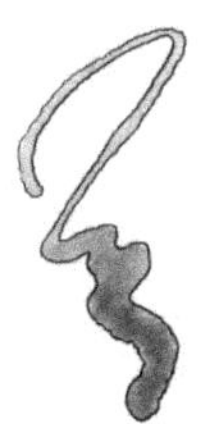

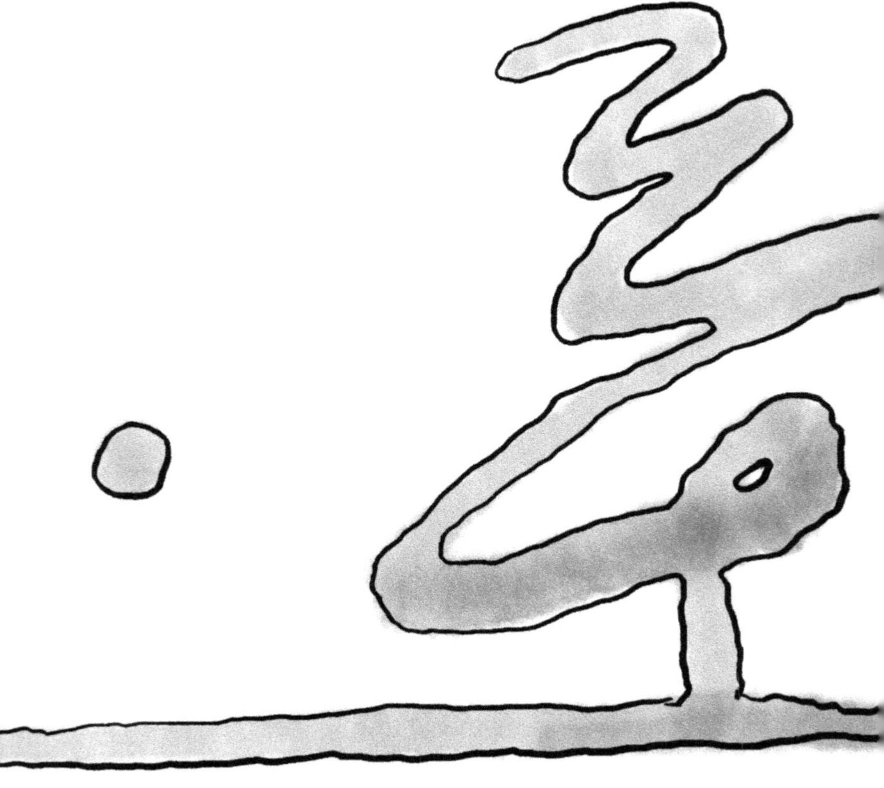

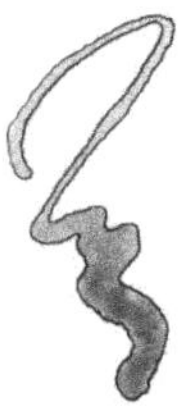

we must say goodbye
it may be a lonely road
leading us back home

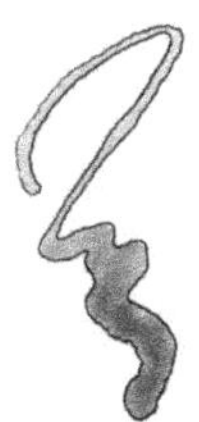

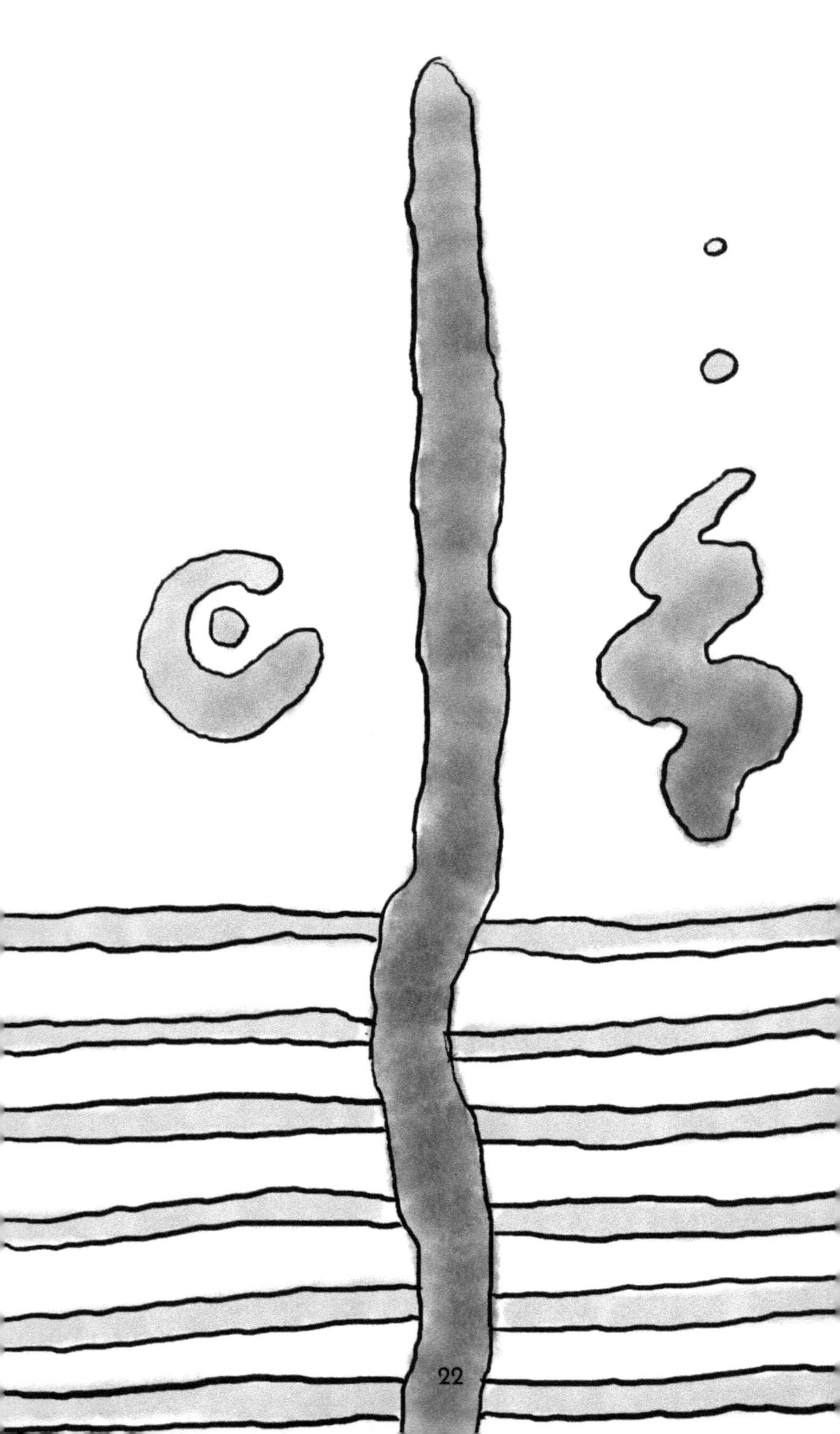

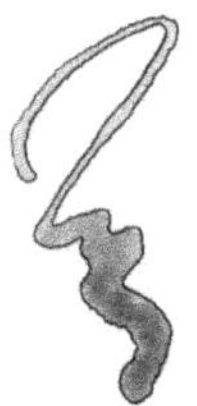

something of the real
a figment of the past dream
discovering now

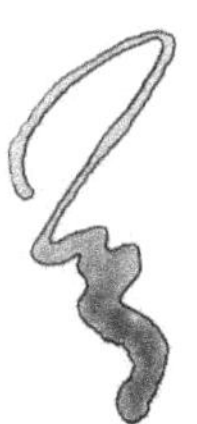

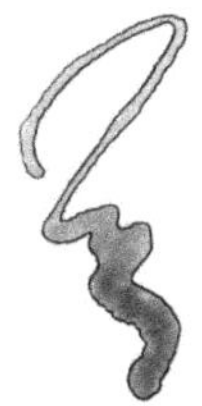

it is all the same

yet it is all disparate

waiting to come home

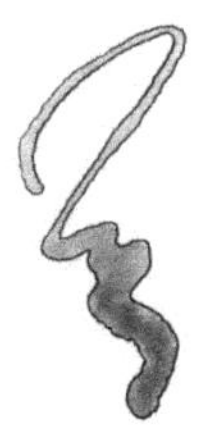

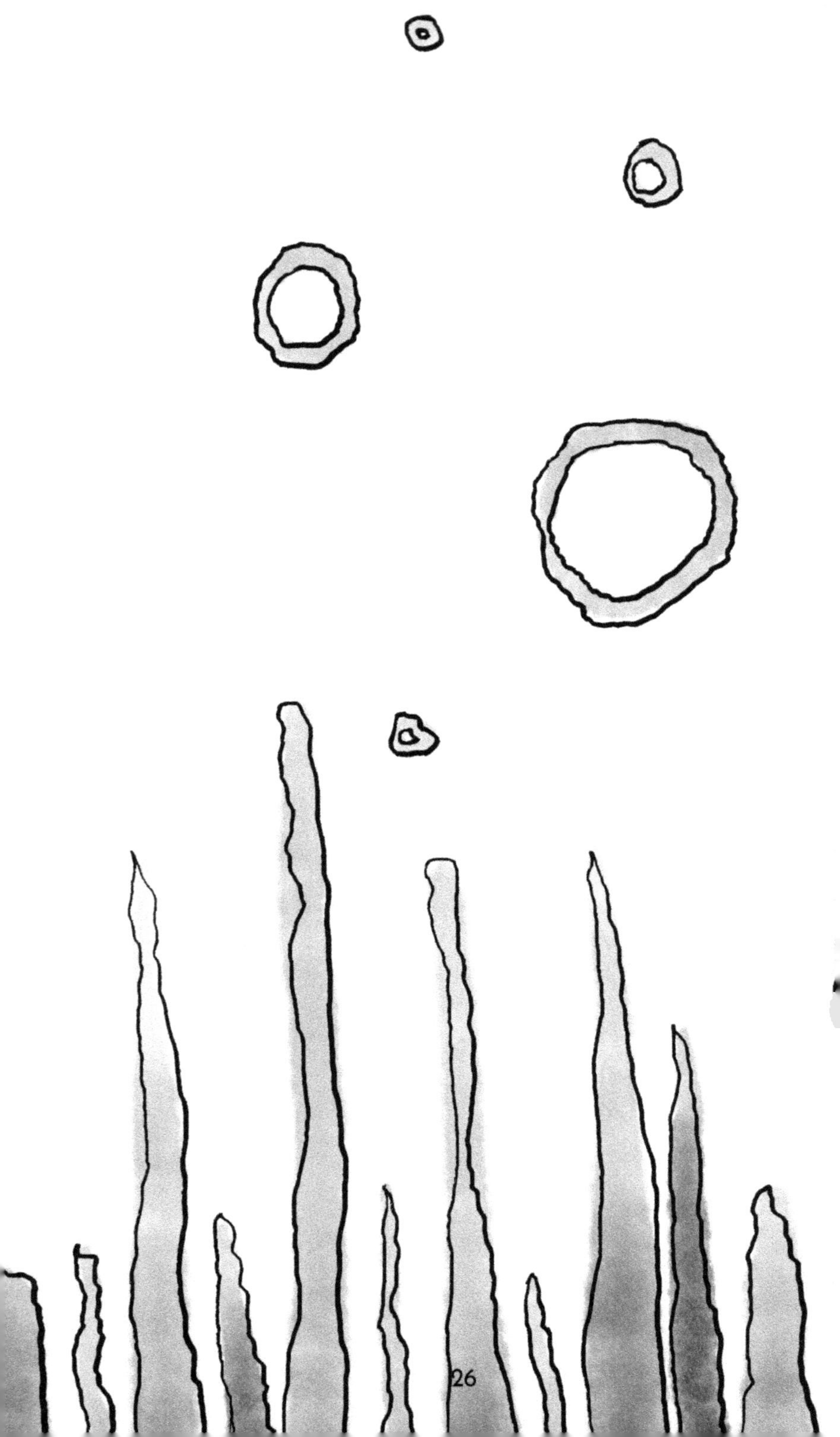

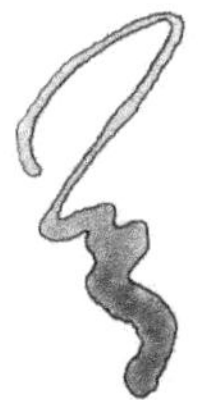

there is hope in us

broken apart but still whole

never have we left

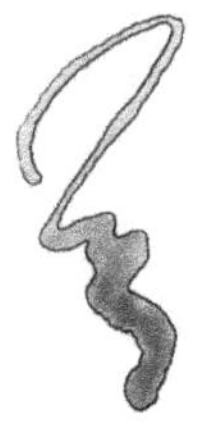

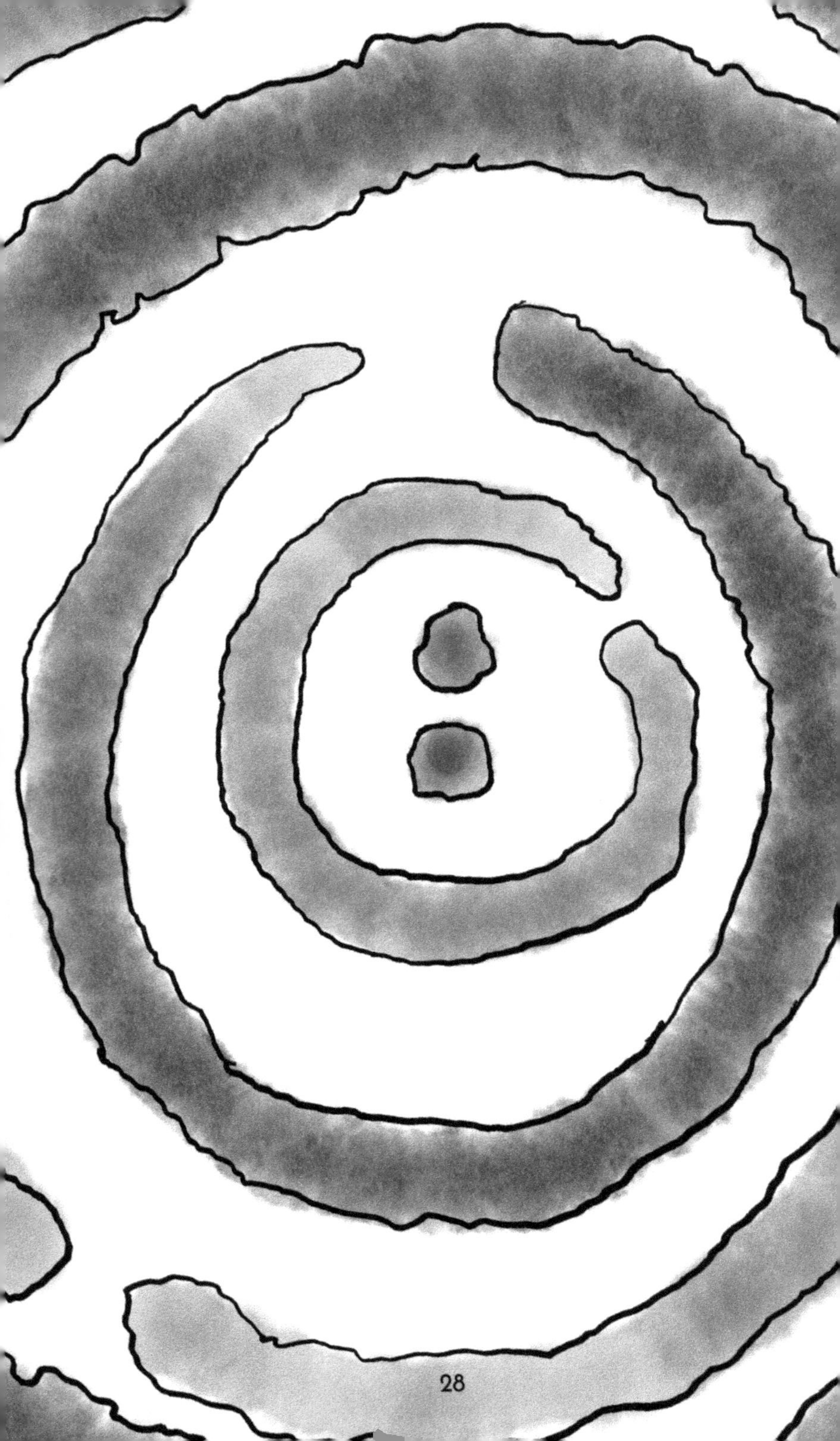

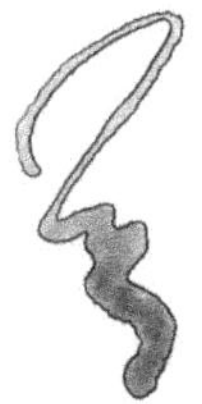

together today

sadness in isolation

no need to be sad

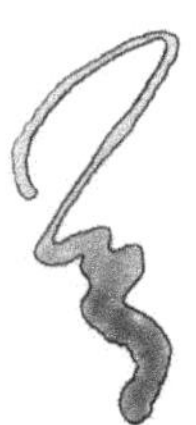

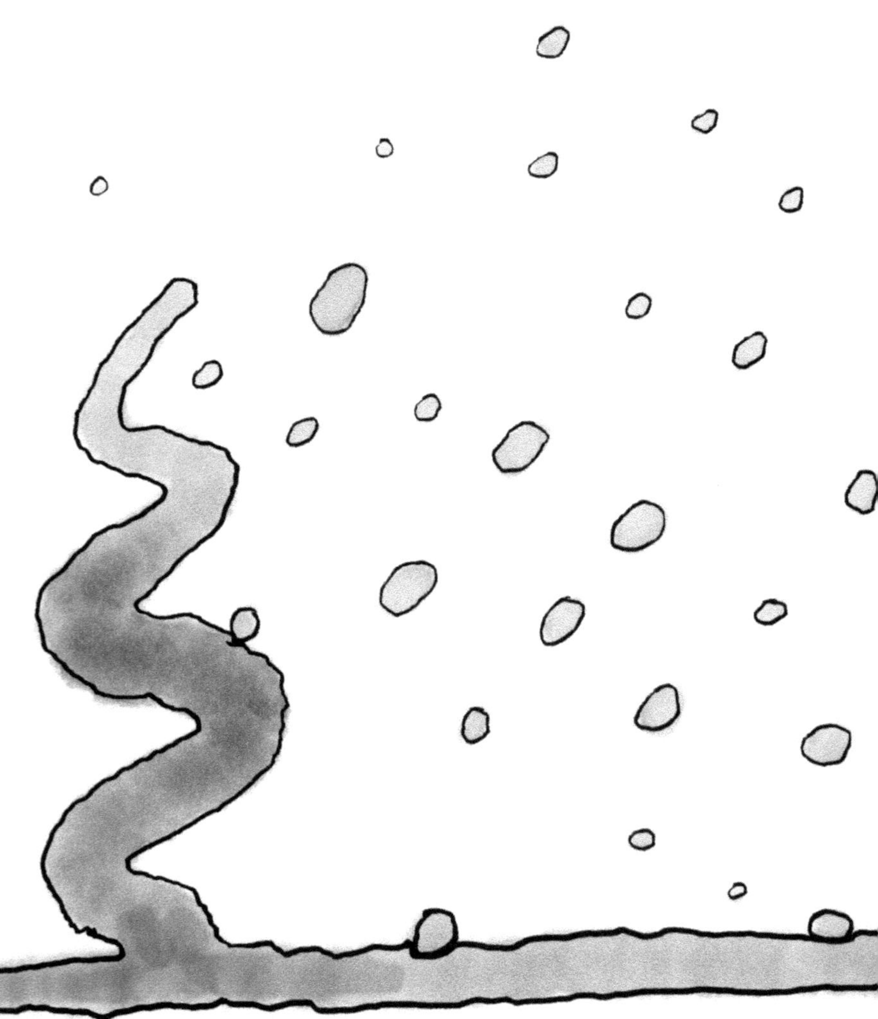

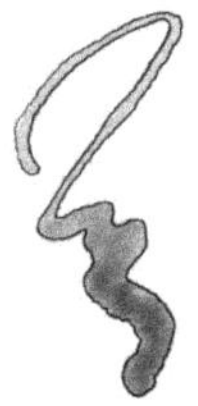

artificial tears

dry in the wind of spirit

bring a sense of calm

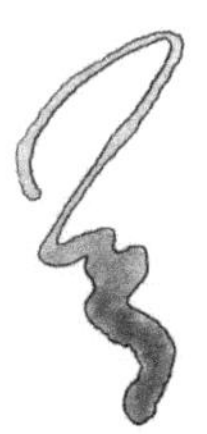

SPACE

gone.

desolation.

empty.

the fabric cries to let the light
spring forth into the endless miracle
of being

we can see the past as our present
rippled and contoured by time
and its brethren

gravity
of space

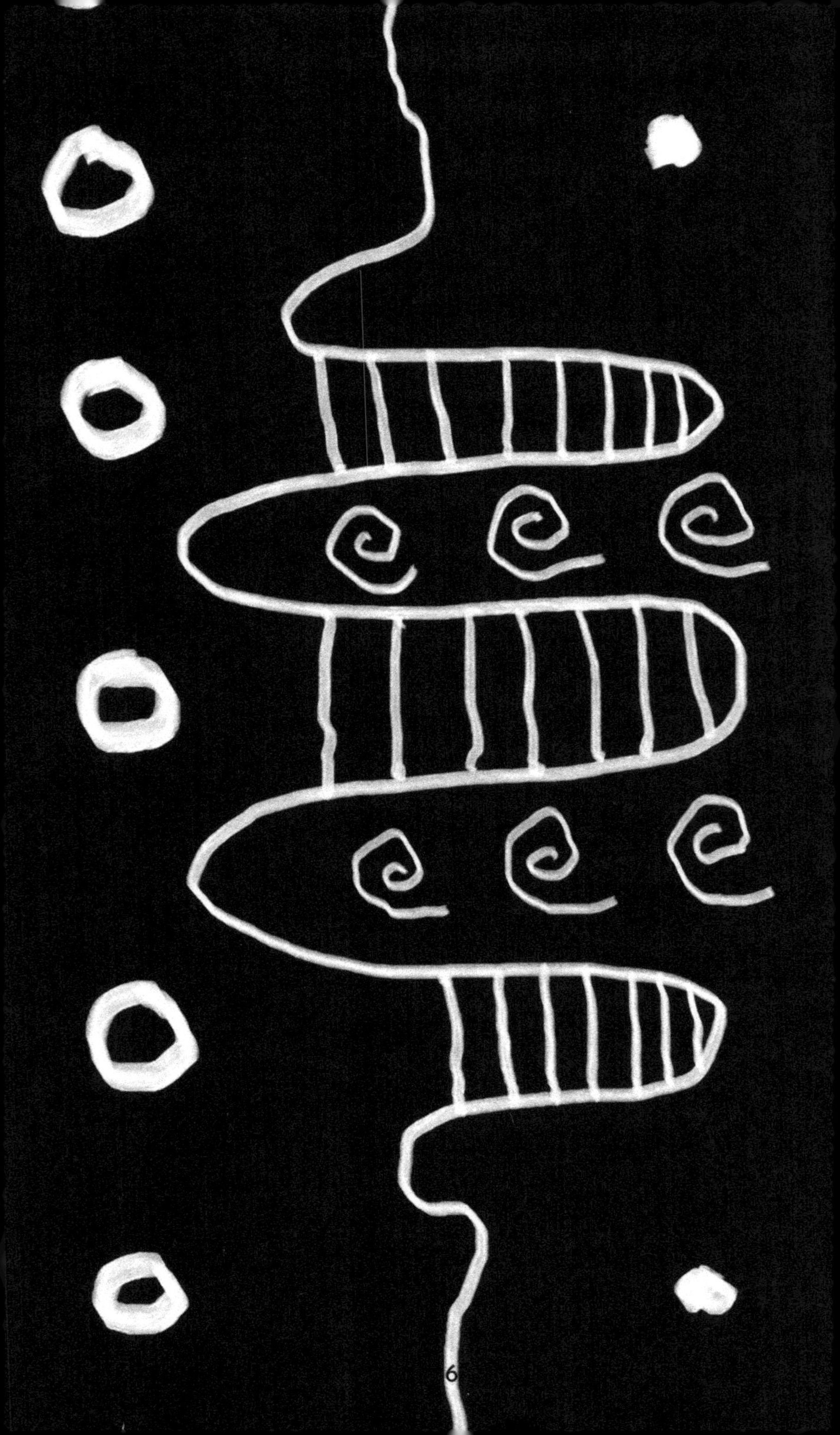

orbs of dust in space
wrestle with the call to join
everyone else

we are not alone
part of the cosmic dancing
radiating here

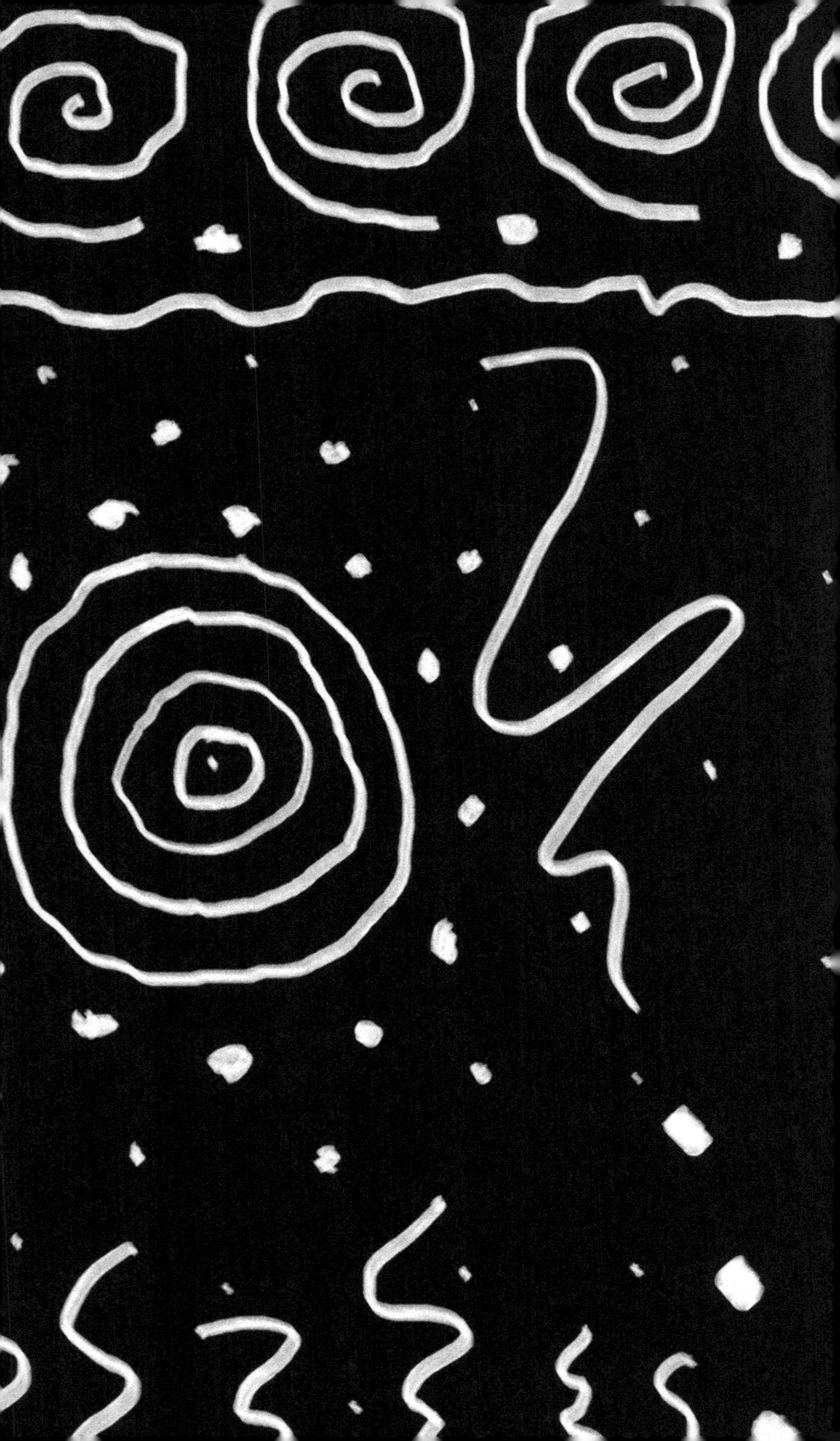

galaxies touch
empty space is but illusion
the embrace is real

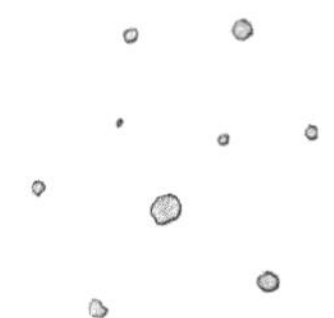

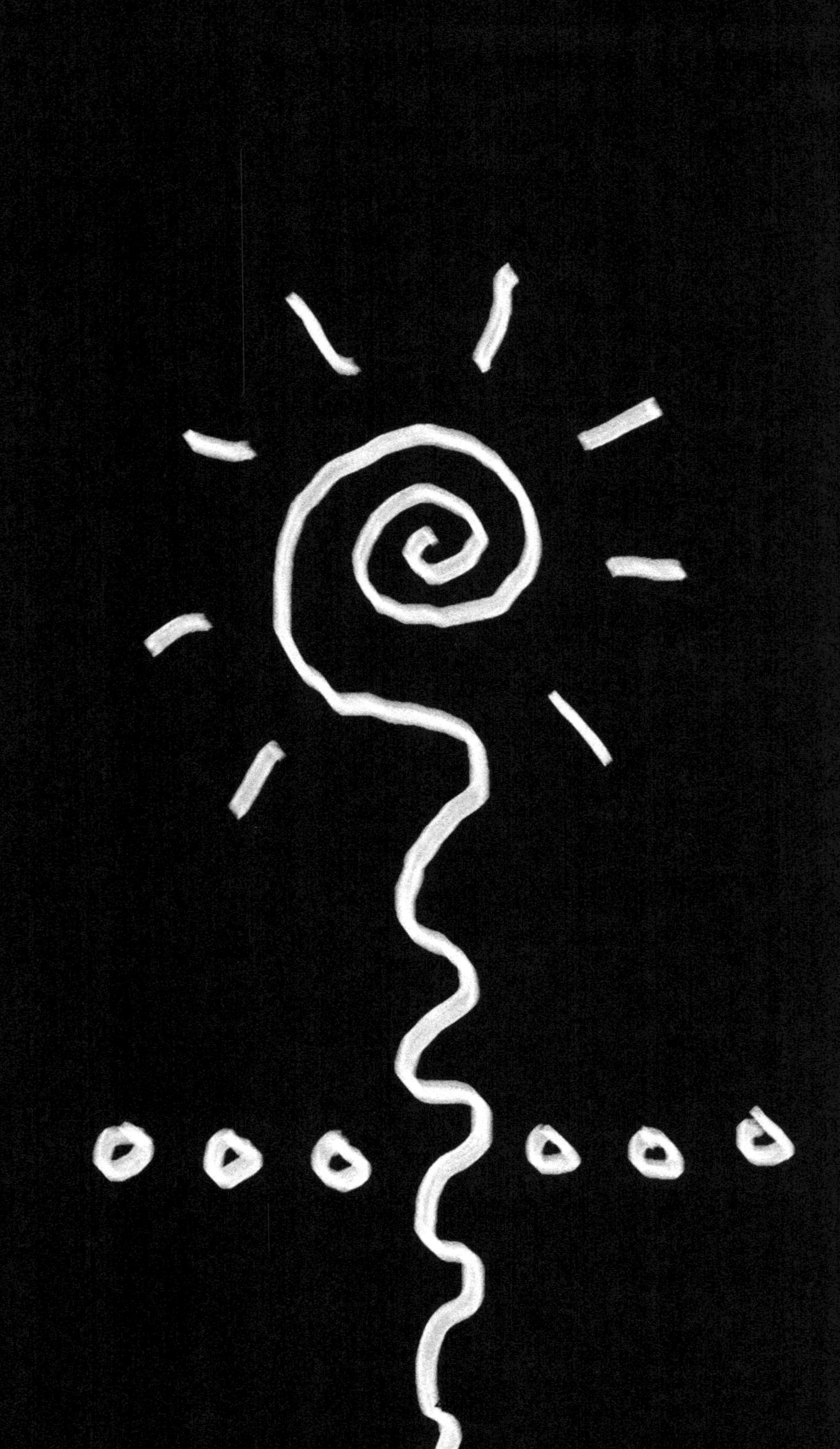

for what it is worth

reaching through the emptiness

to hold on for grace

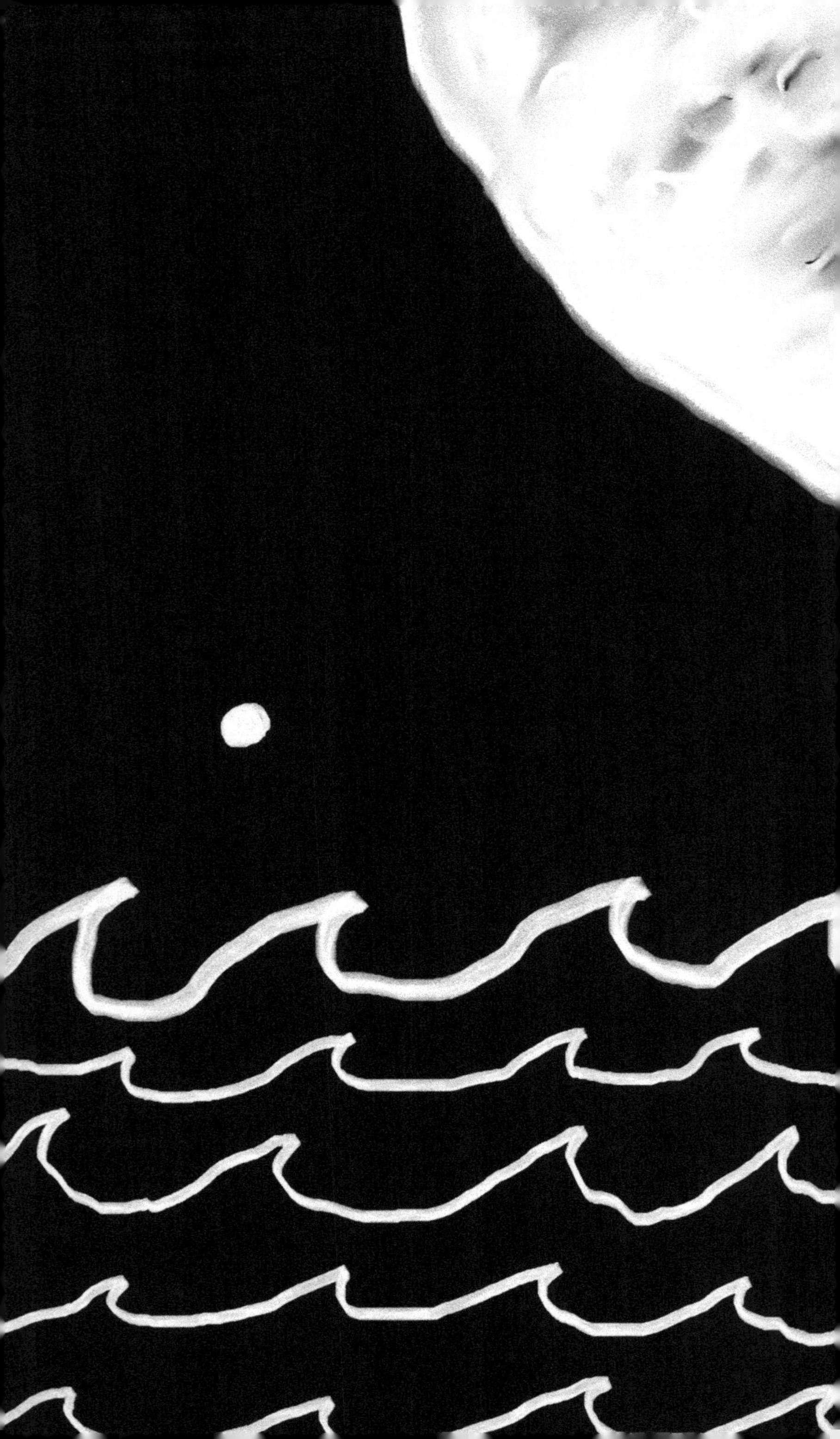

the moon shines for us

the tide rises to greet it

only to retreat

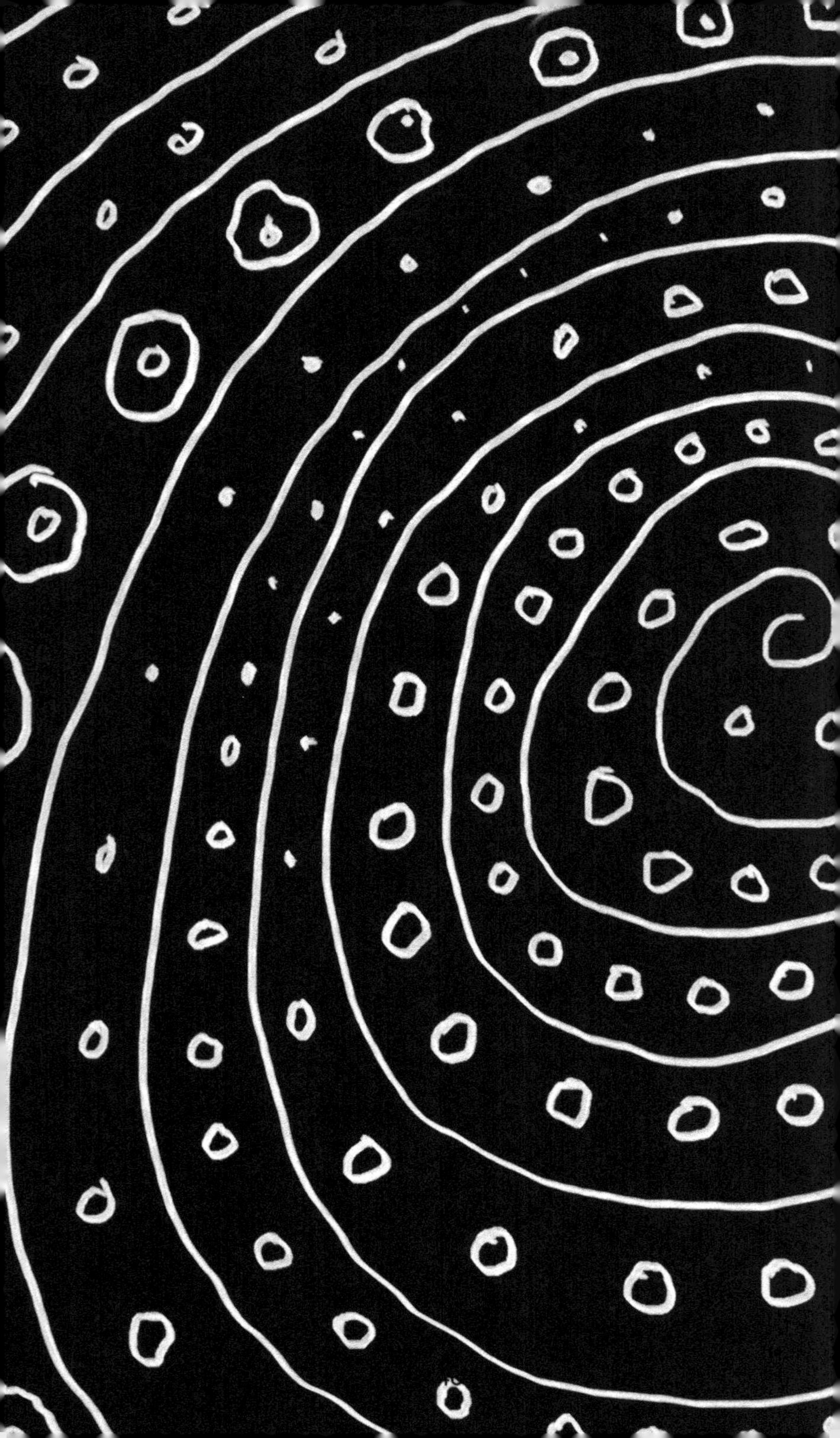

look out at it all

look in at everything

one in it's sameness

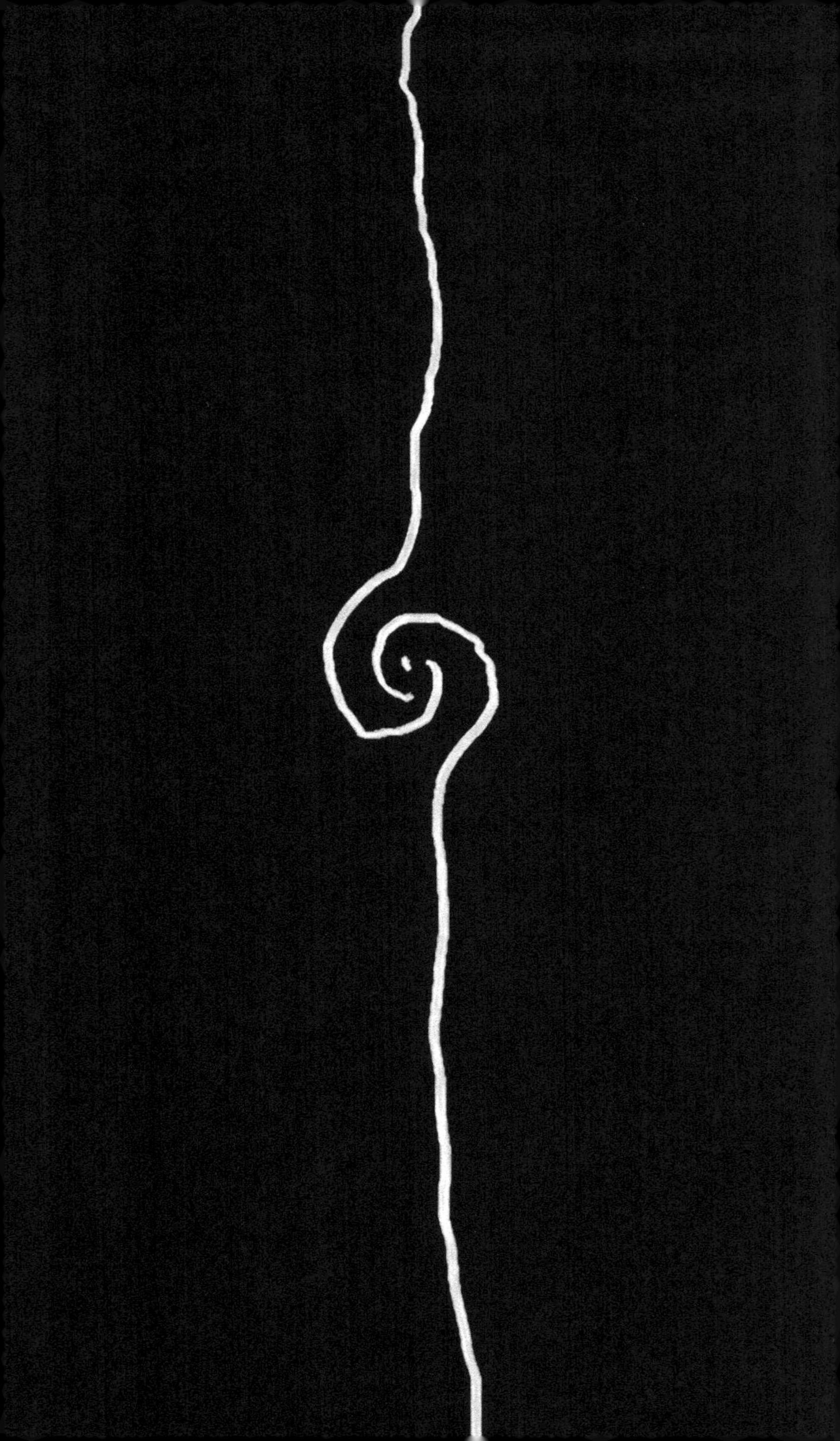

the dance of the light
pulled around the celestial
meeting with us all

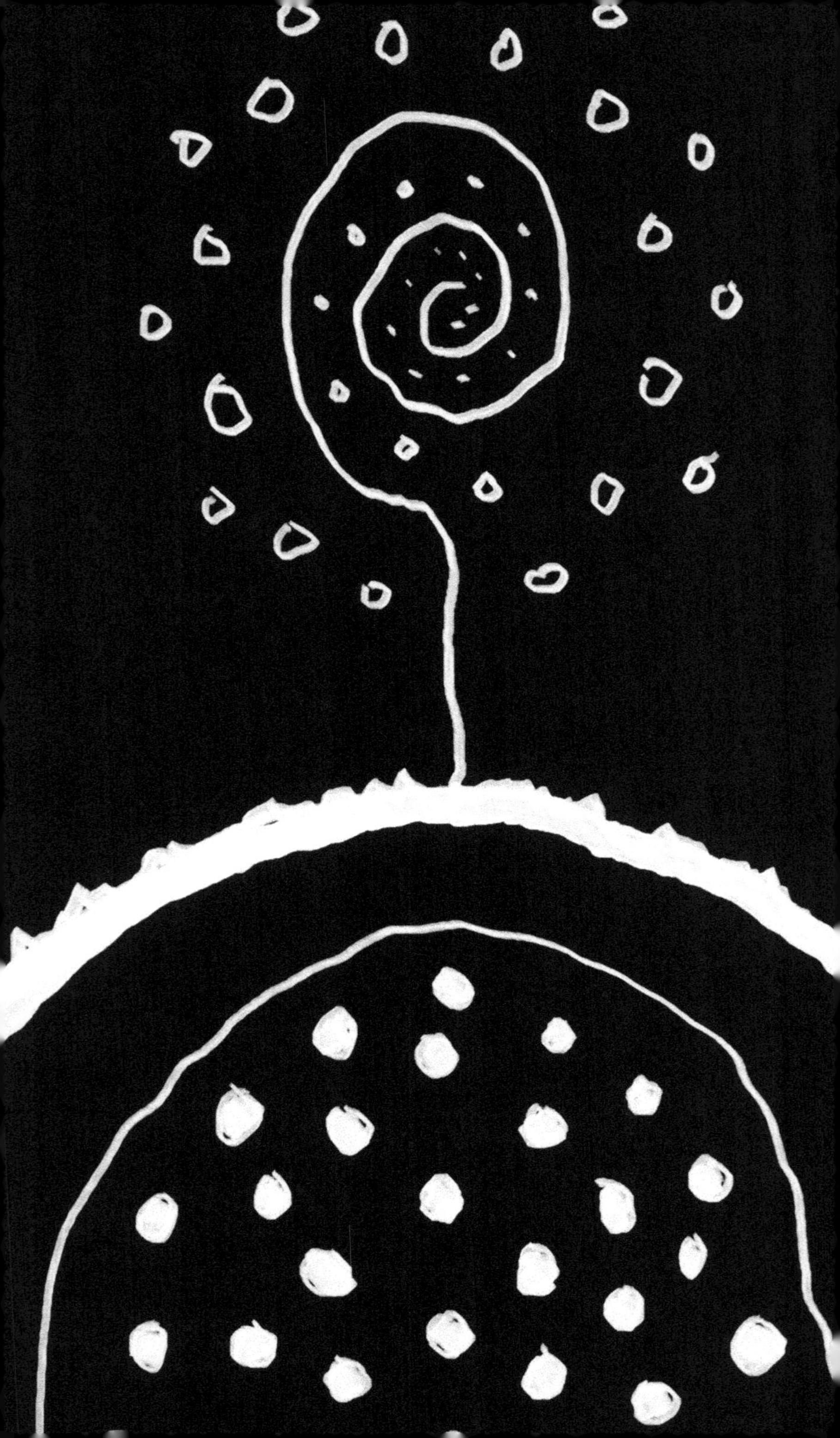

a mere spec we are
converging with all our kin
holding hands with god

FEAR

do you see it in my eyes
there is something that speaks to us
all at times

lurking like a thief who sees the
opportunity to line their pockets

emptying the contents of your soul
on the ground to be picked through

though the thief is just a mirage
we kneel before them
awaiting our fate

gravity of fear

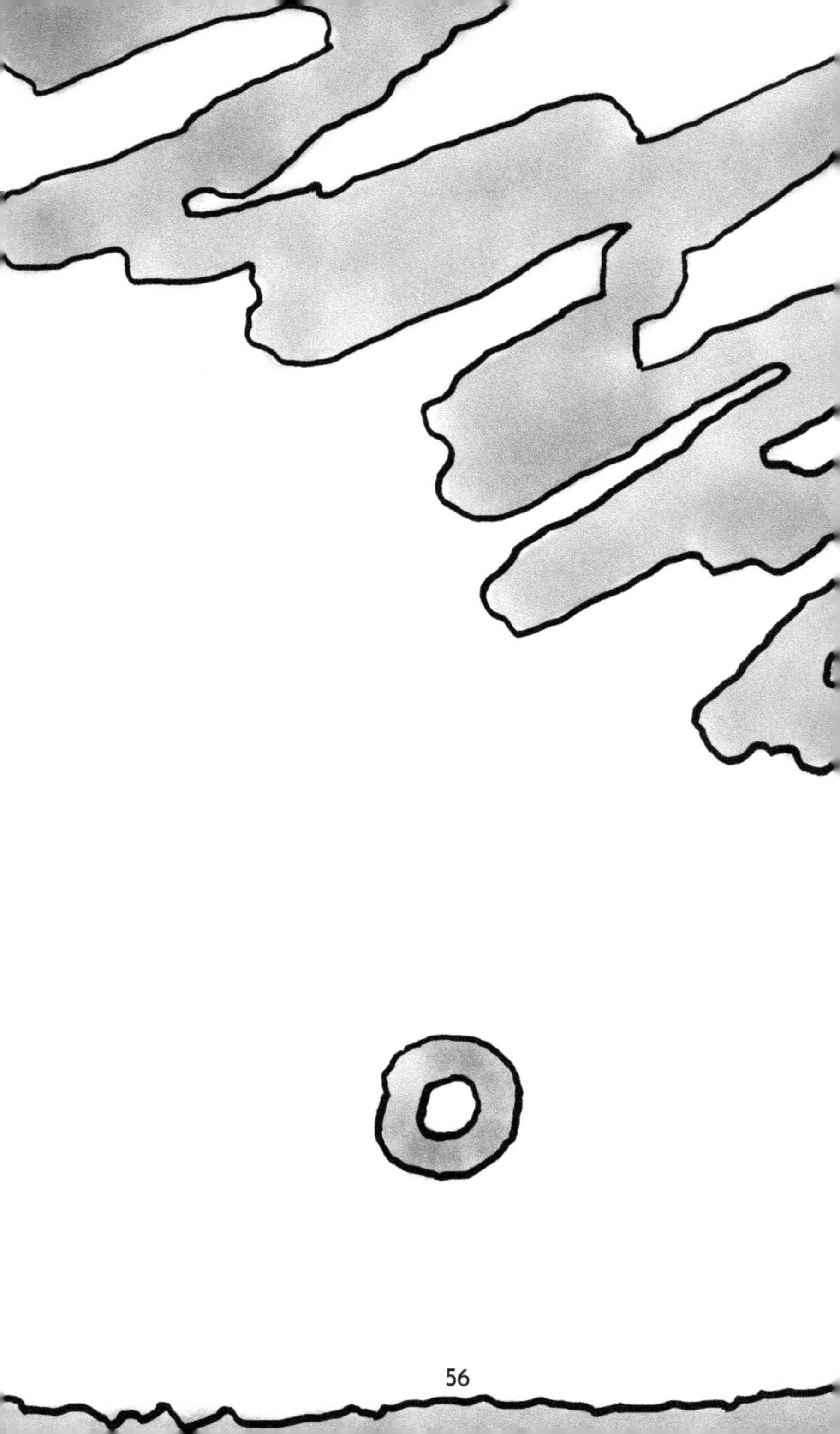

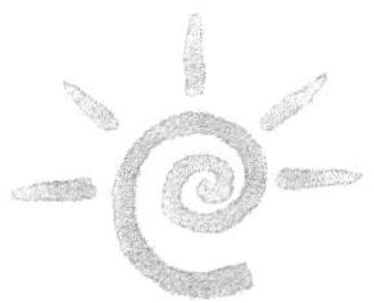

never has peace been
under the sky we shall see
known is the outcome

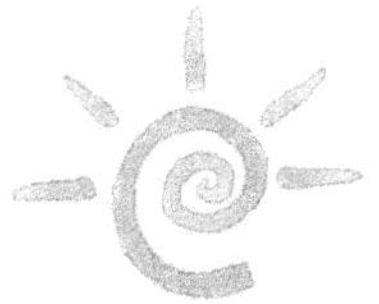

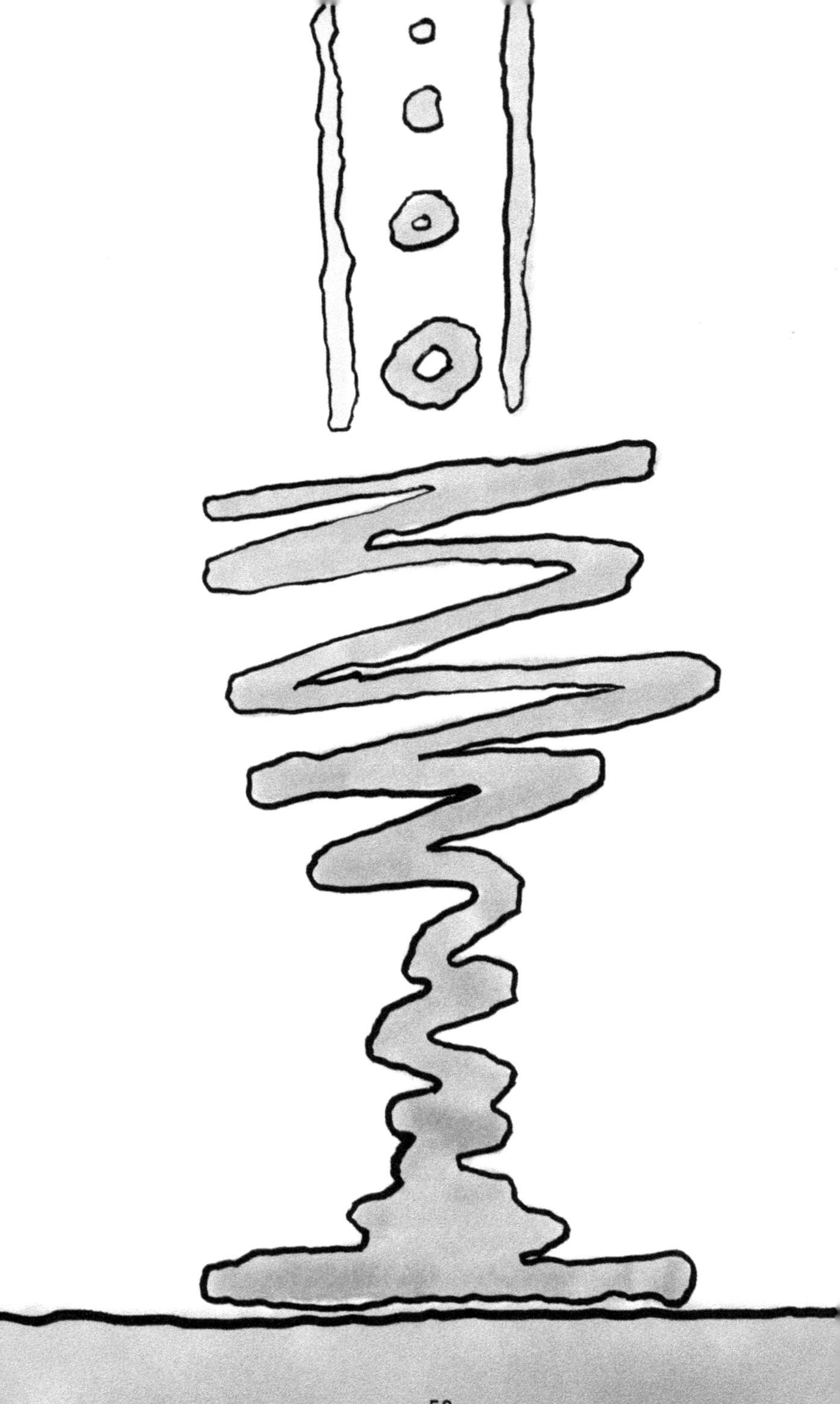

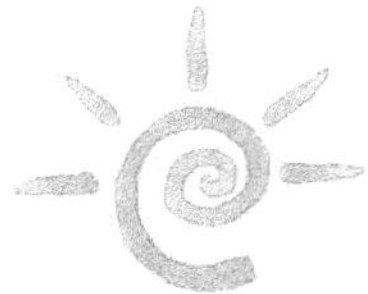

take my cup today
bring it back in the morning
waiting with nothing

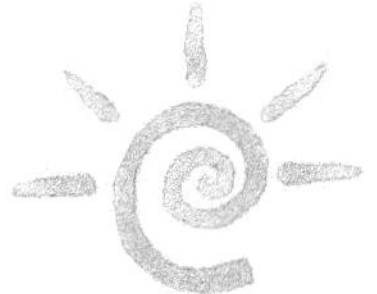

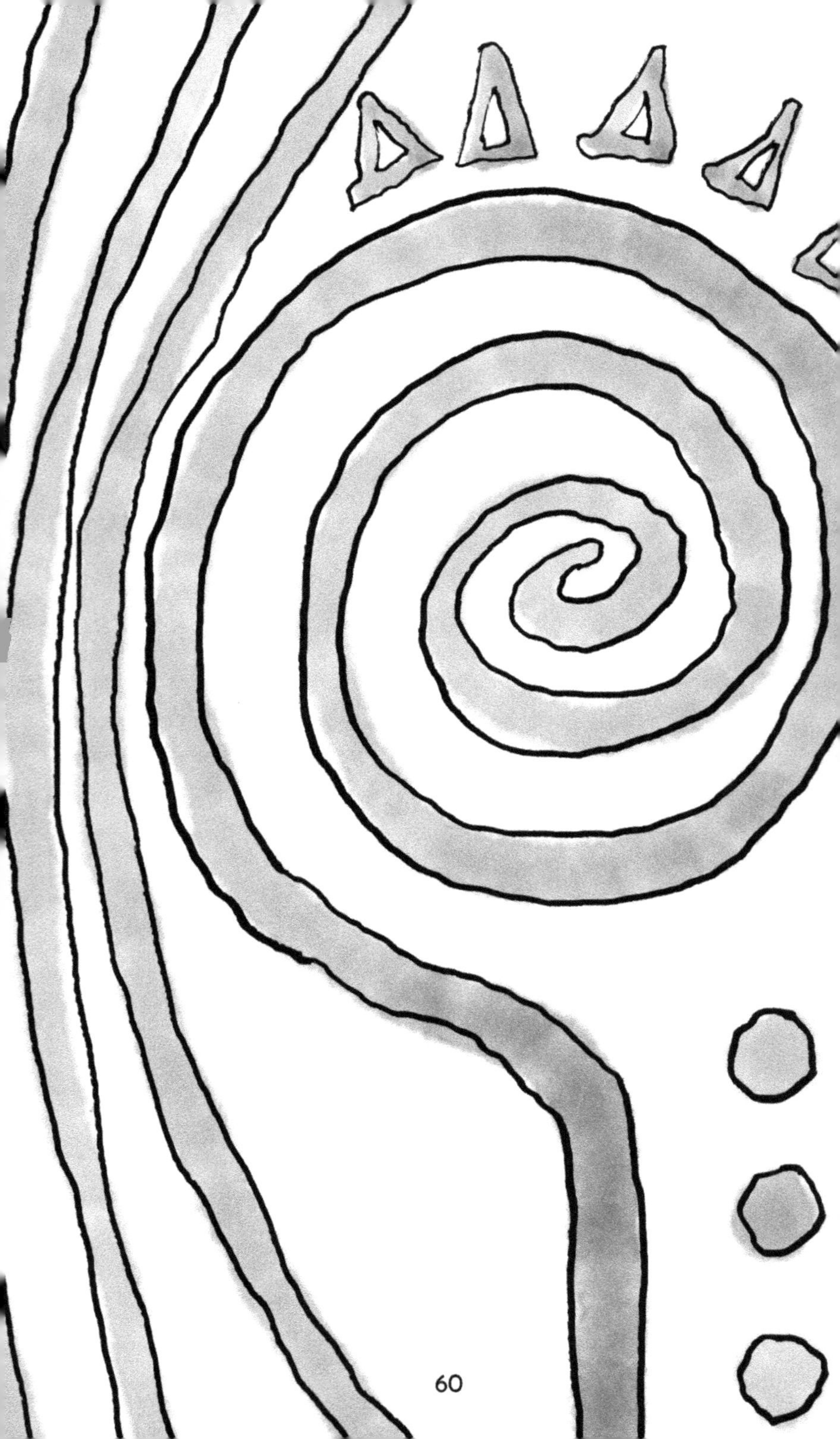

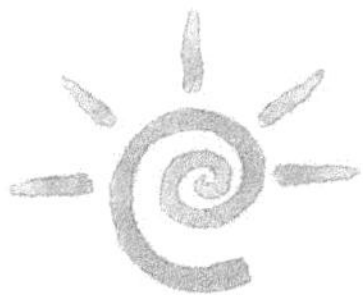

harboring feelings
of discontented vagrants
try to stop the wind

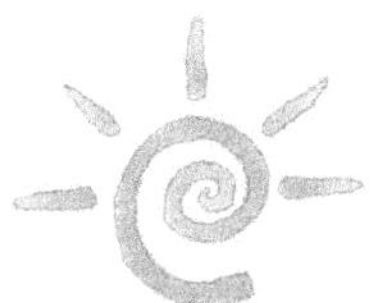

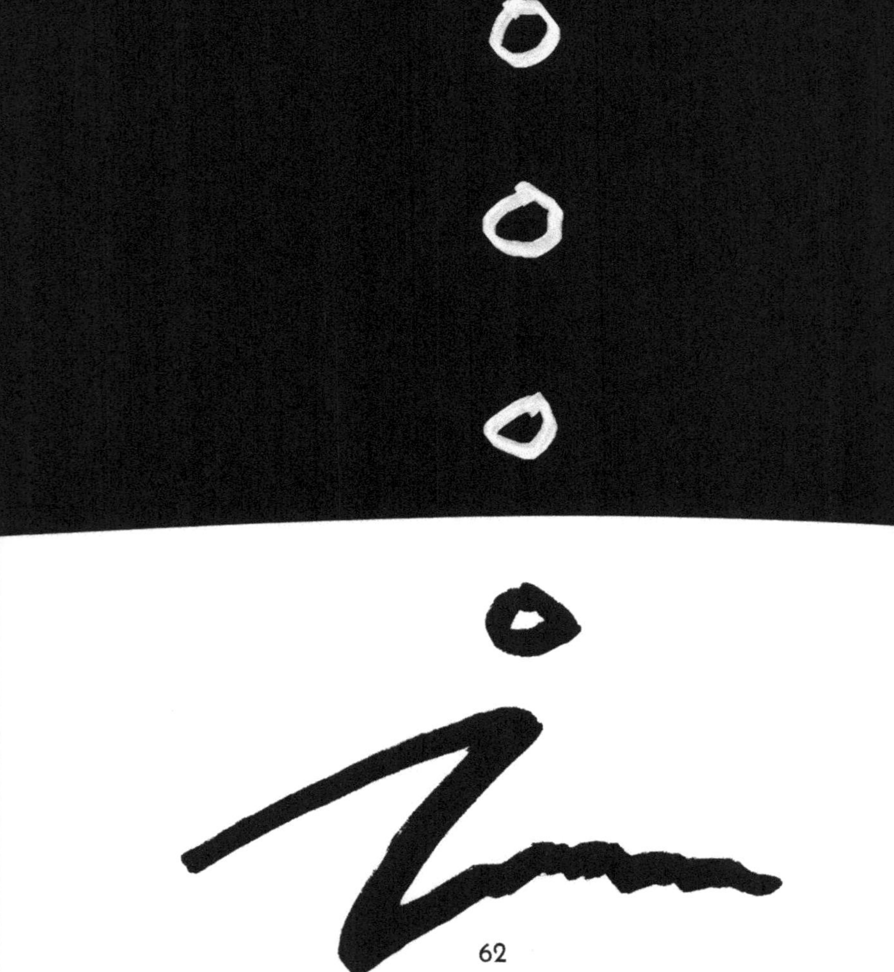

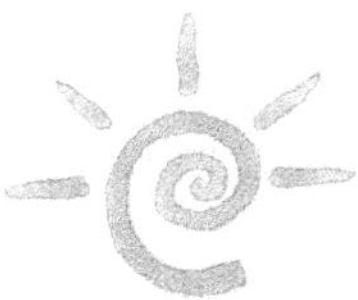

make me feel something
breaking upon the night sky
my mind has left me

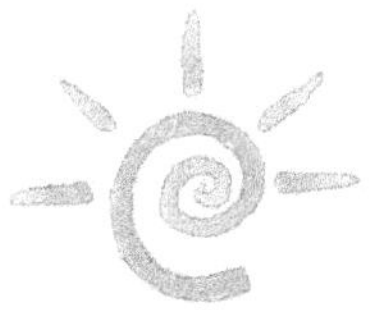

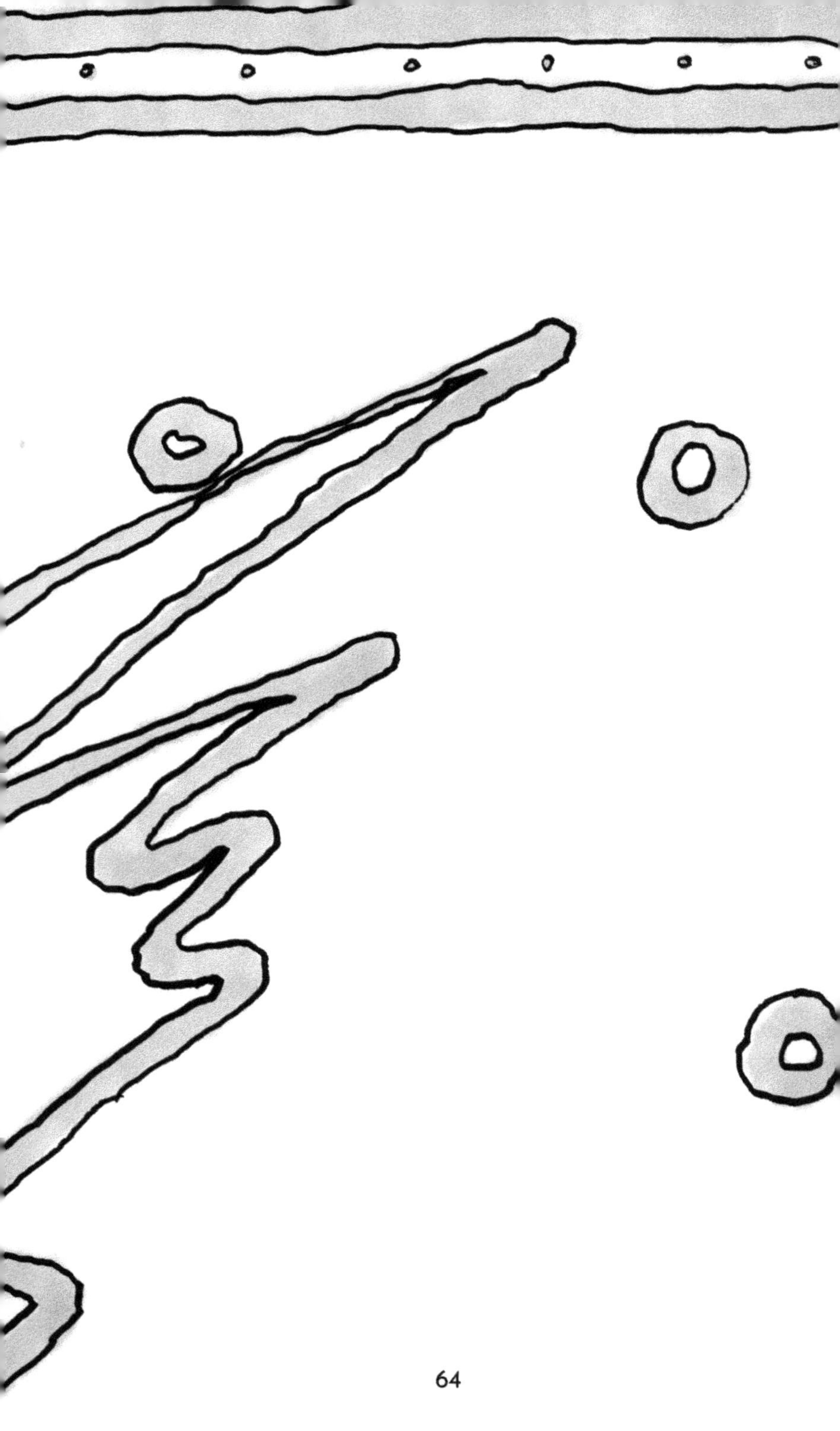

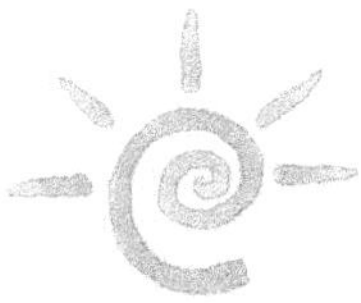

losing the essence

taking a chance on the grift

only to see loss

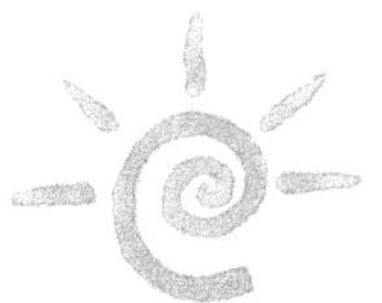

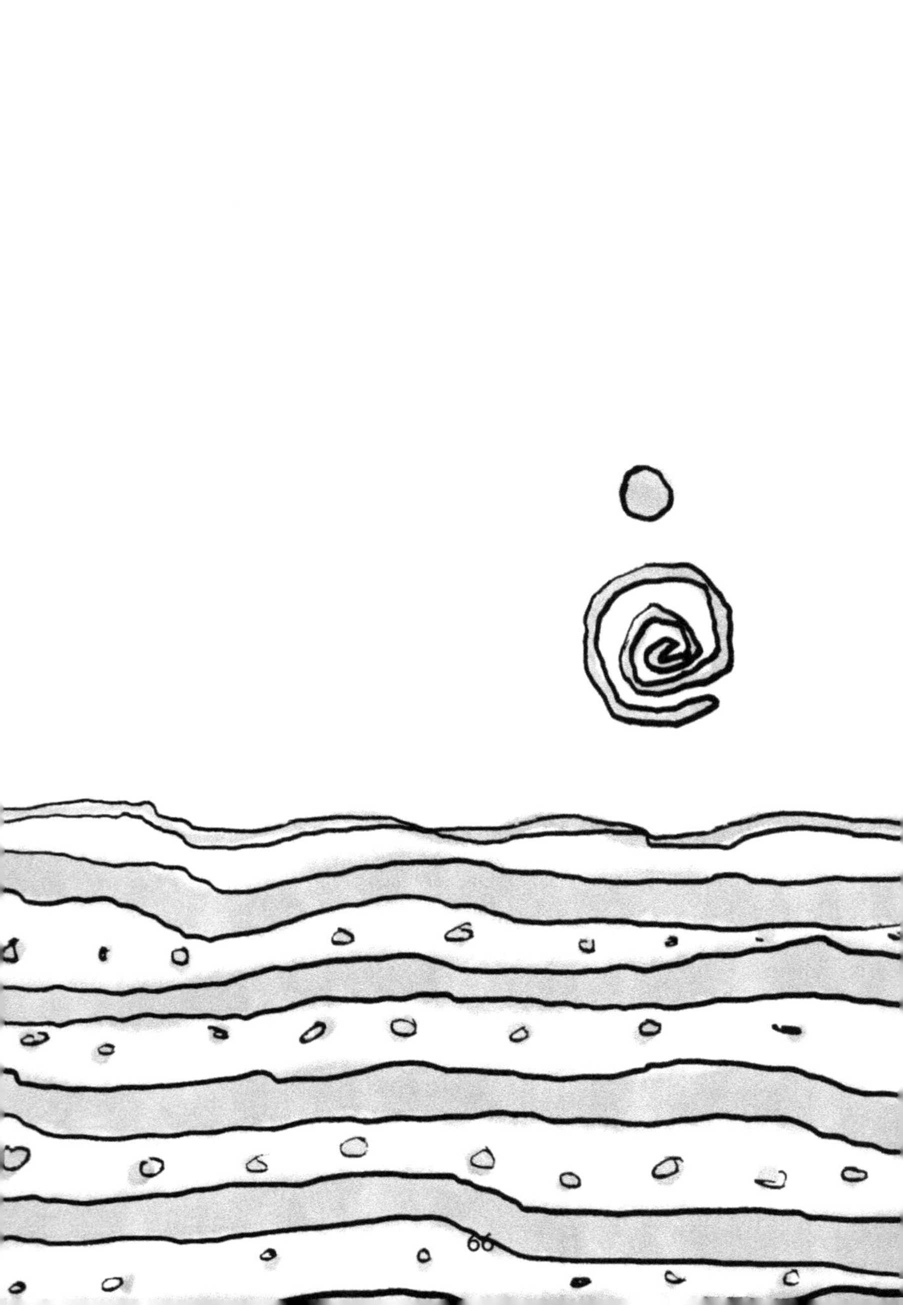

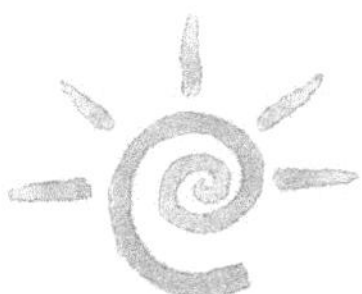

drifting from senses
lost in a sea of ether
endless possibilities

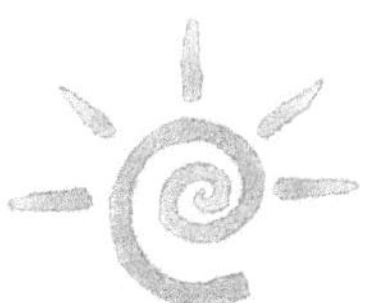

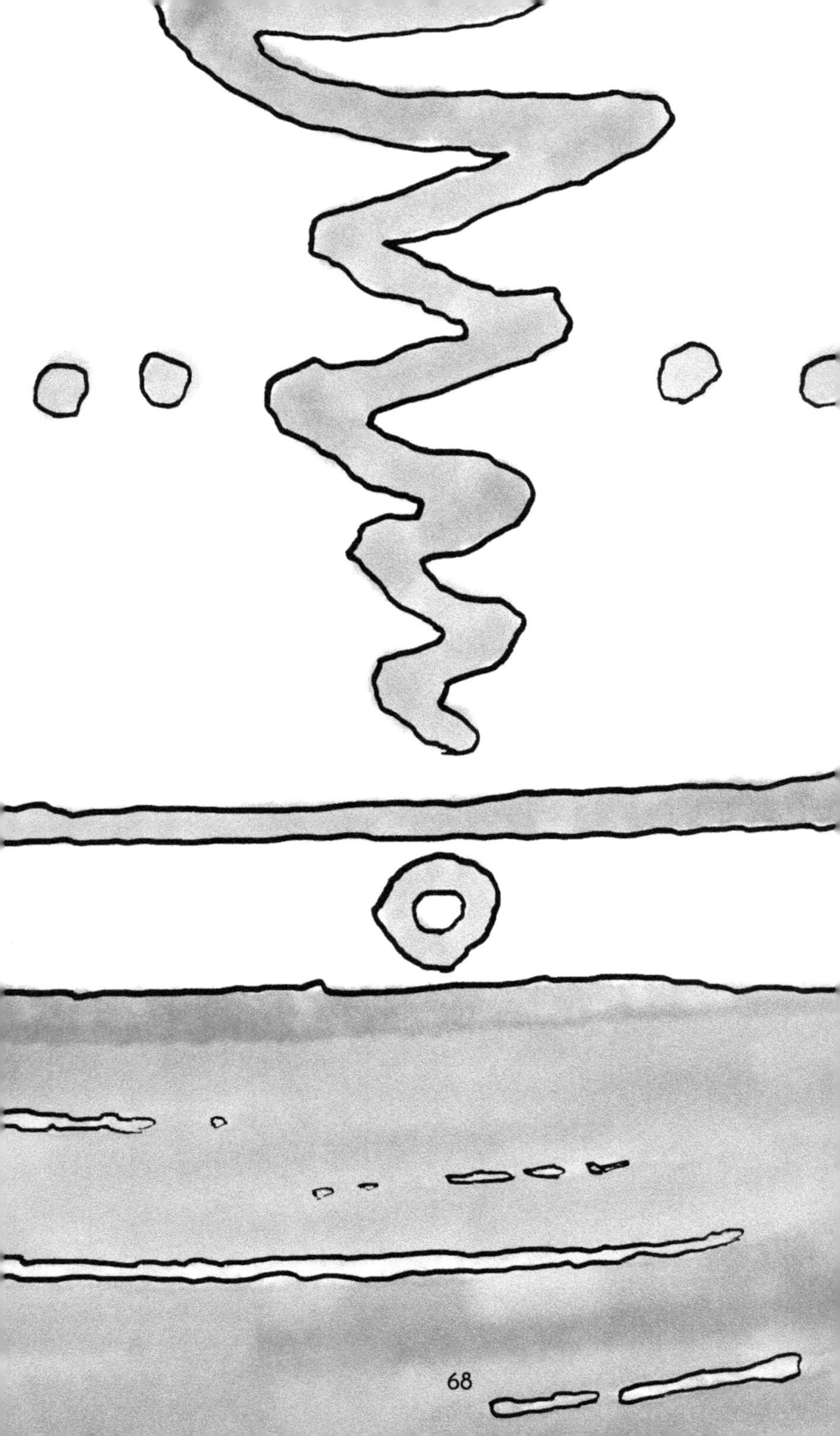

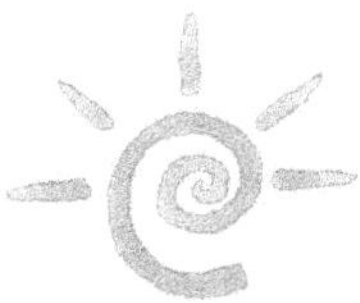

shattered on the ground
but still whole on this table
together but gone

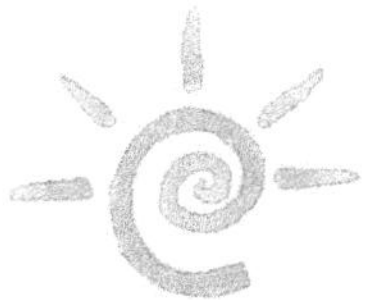

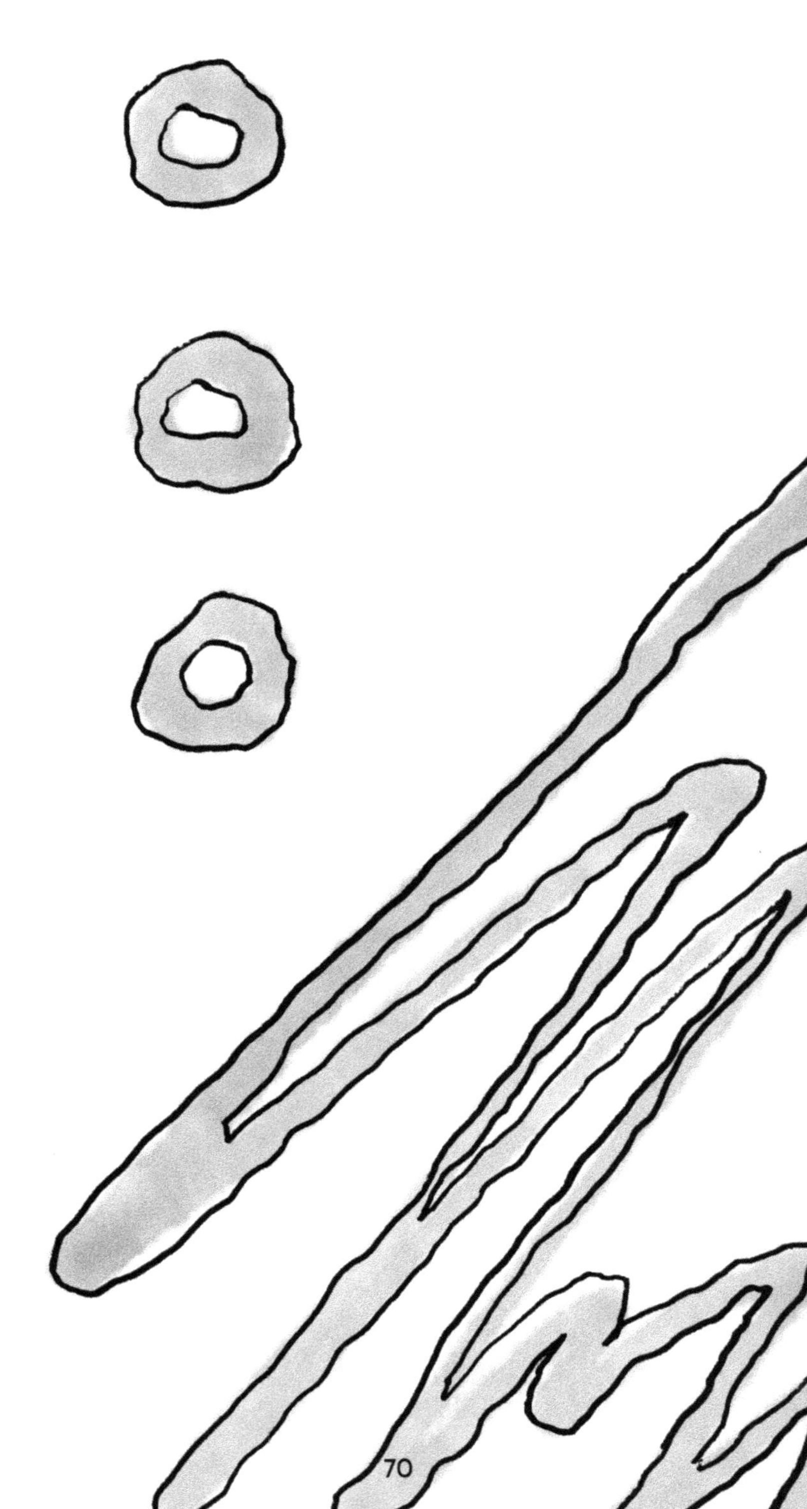

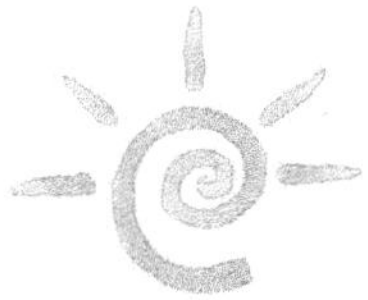

there are times we fail

in the anticipation

hides the preamble

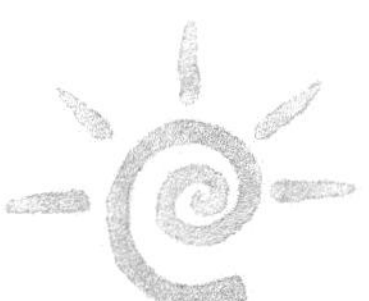

EARTH

growing beyond the bounds
reaching plateaus of grandeur
amongst the foliage

the balancing act grows weary of
maintaining the posture of life

drawing downward
the majestic lifeblood
is left withering on the ground
waiting to rise again

gravity
of earth

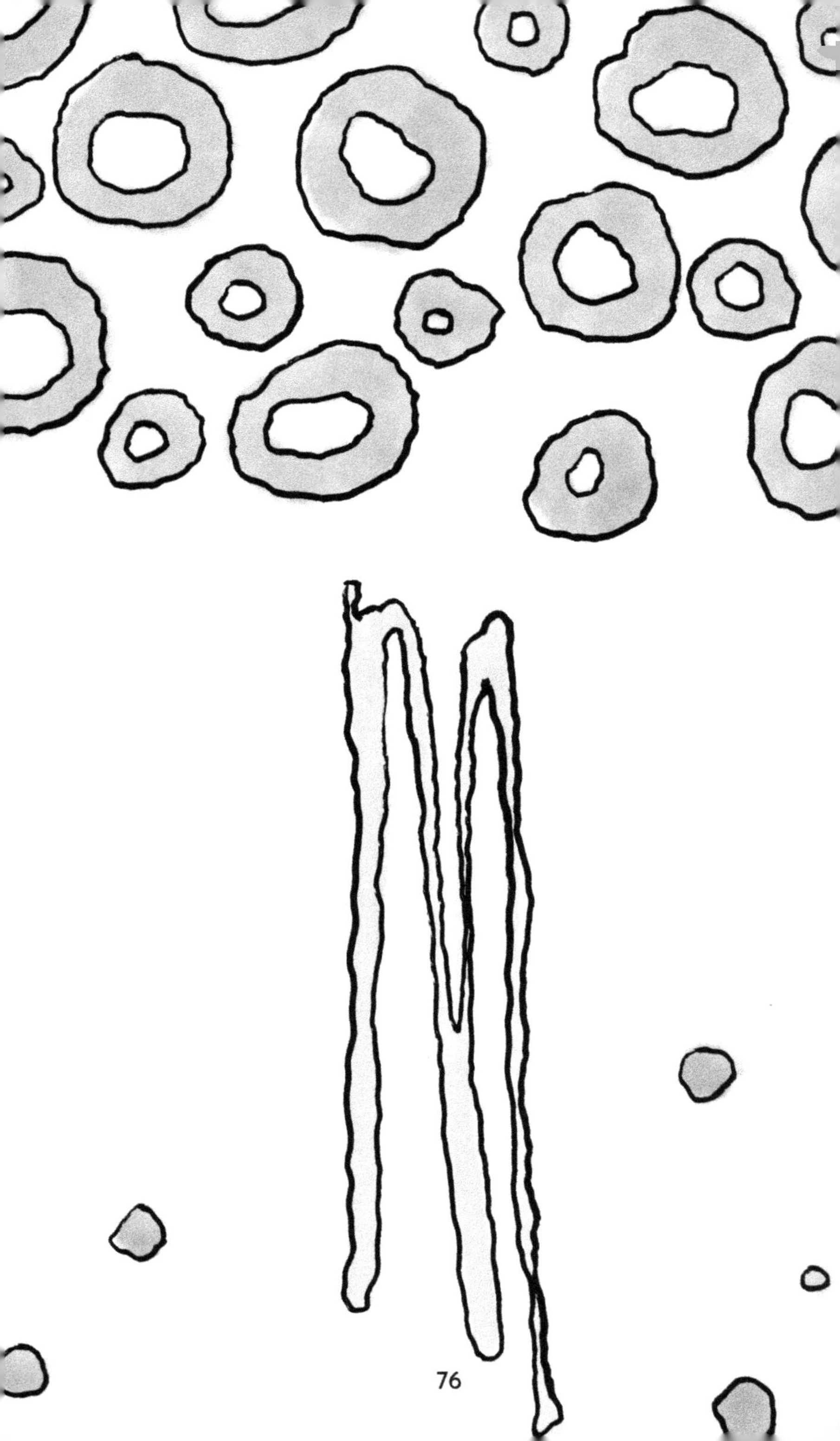

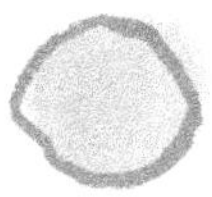

falling from the tree
declaration of being
no more mystery

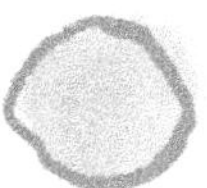

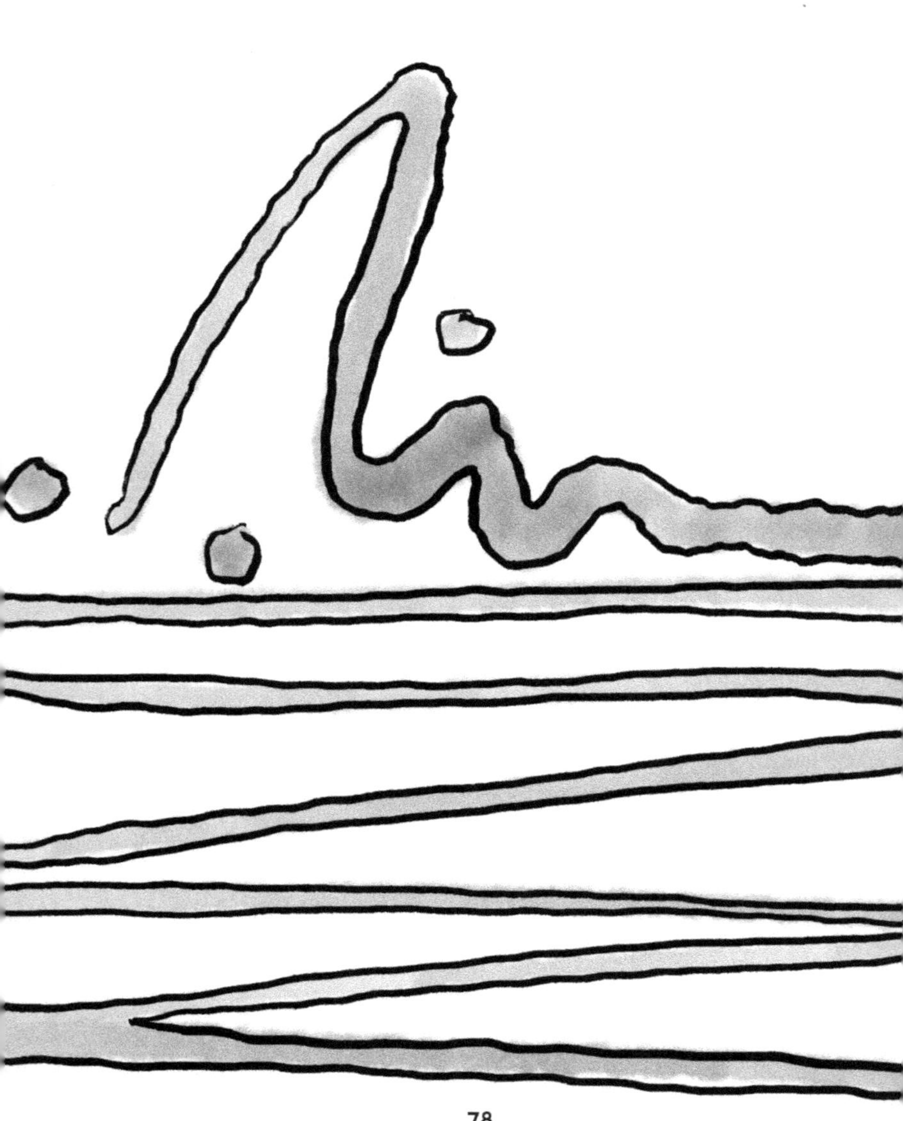

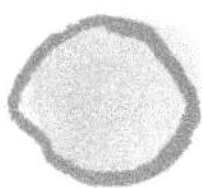

attracted downward
no possible place to go
there we shall take rest

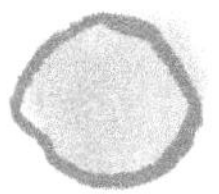

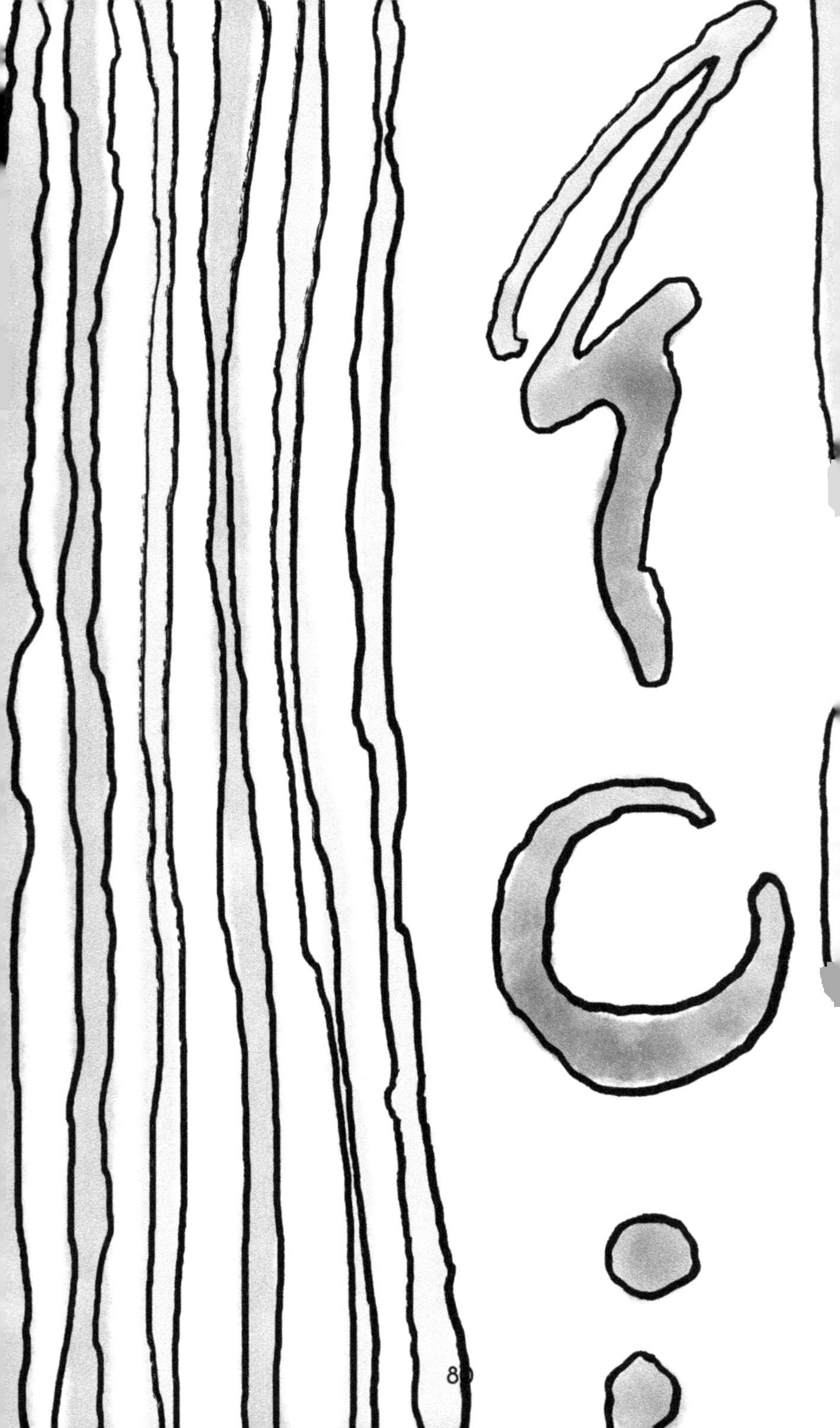

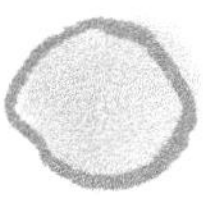

we see the unseen
moving without a reason
resting with no rest

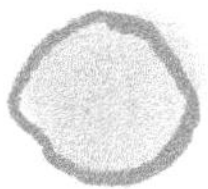

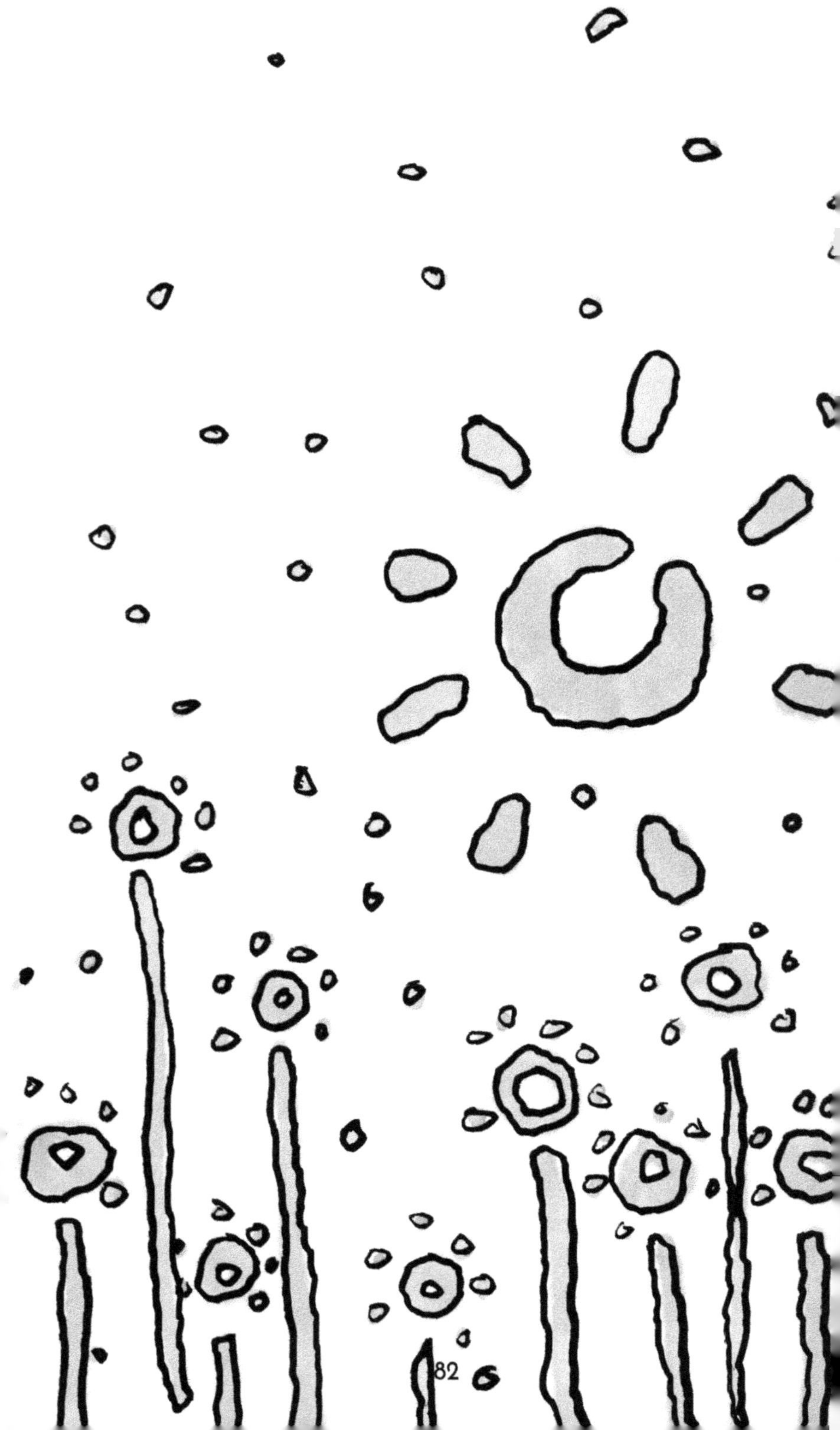

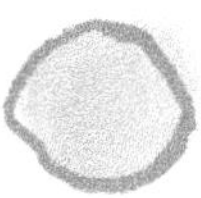

leaping for the sun

waiting to see if they fly

rejoining the earth

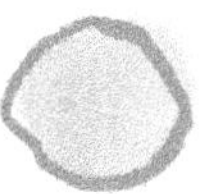

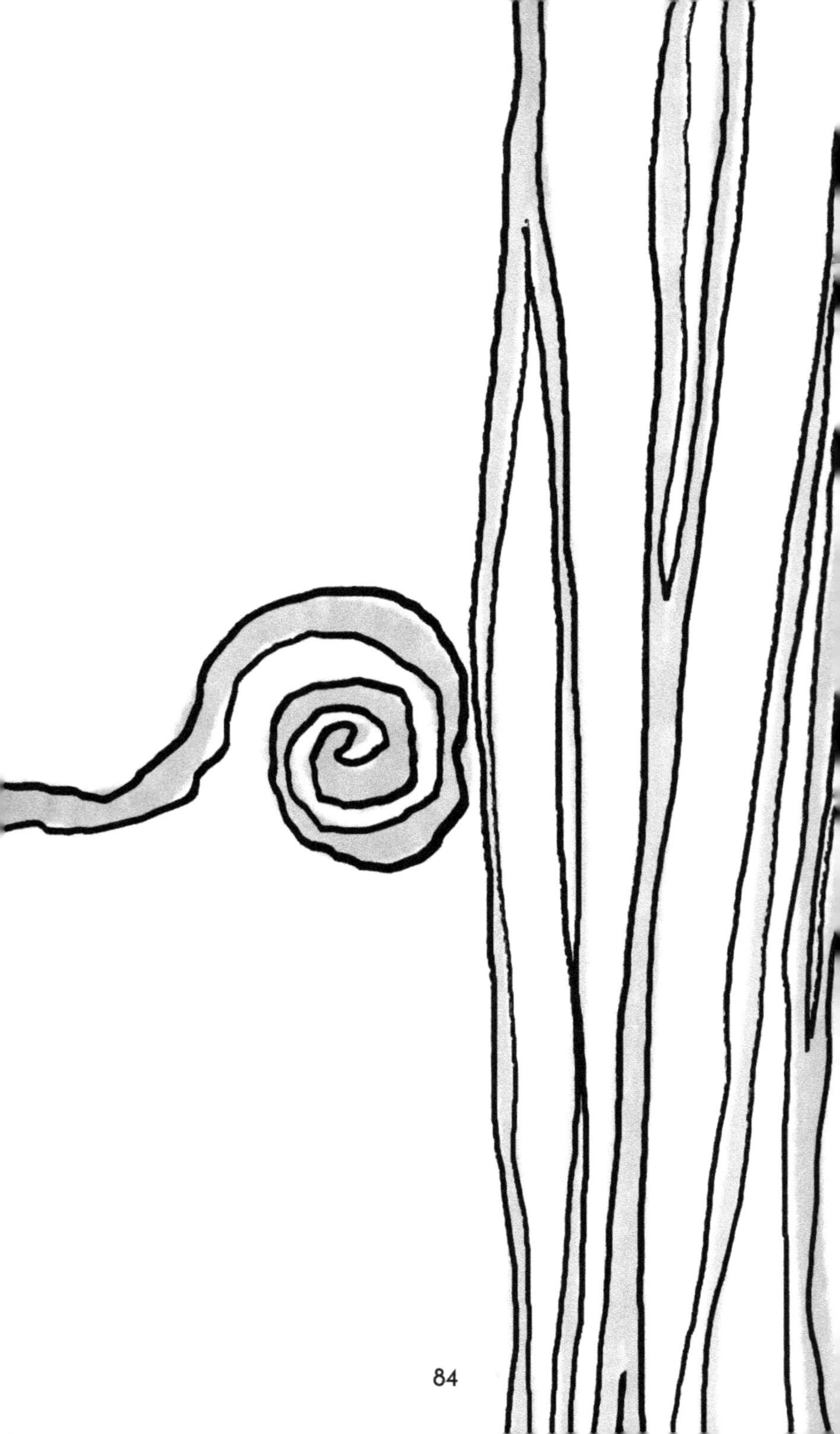

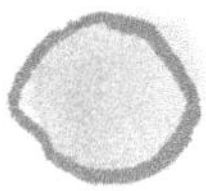

immense attraction

brings particles together

joining the broken

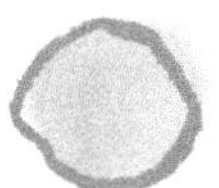

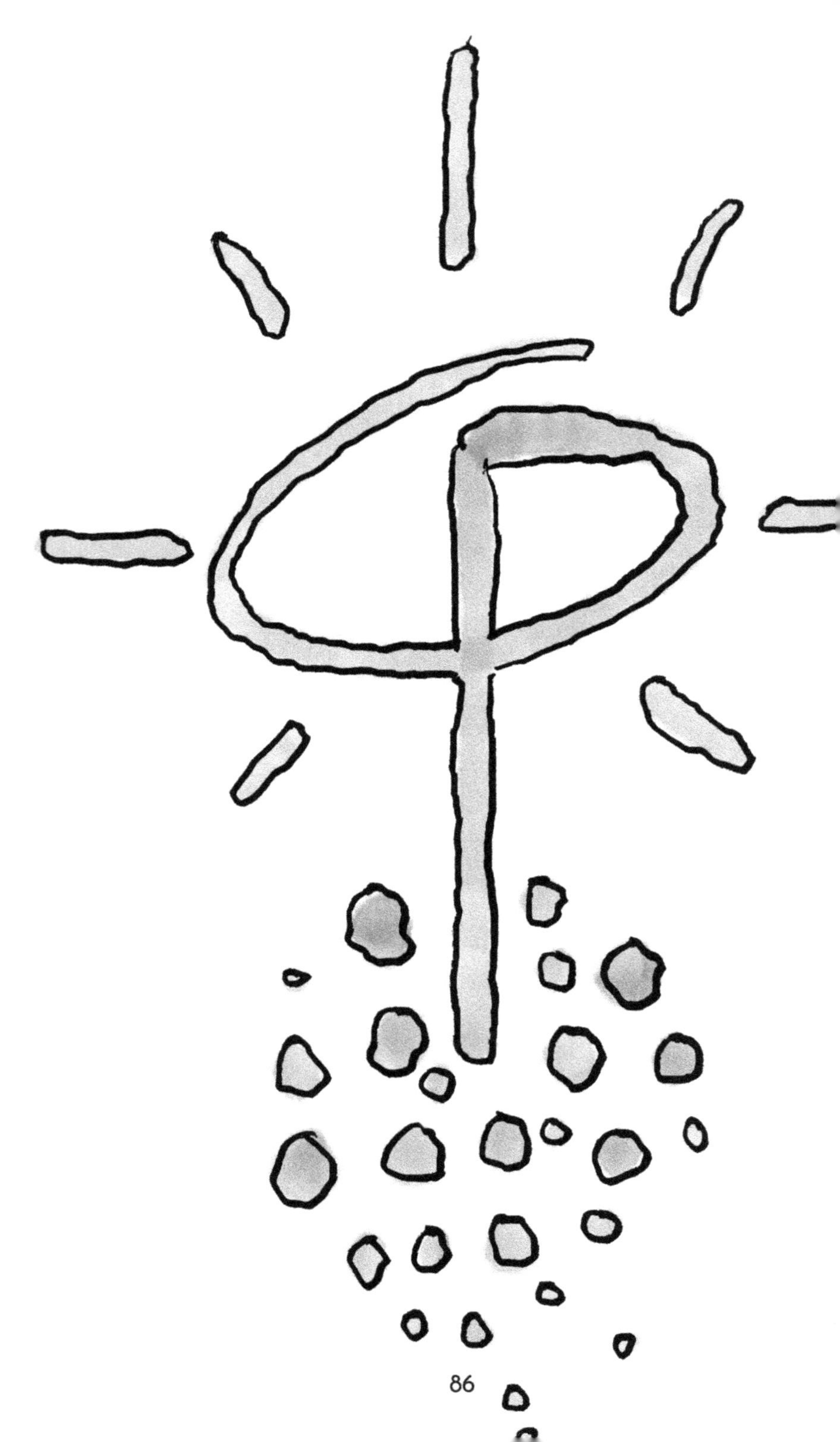

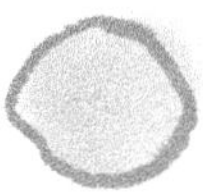

once moving away

now stable in the balance

only to succumb

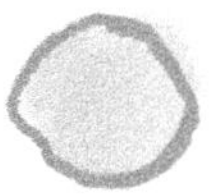

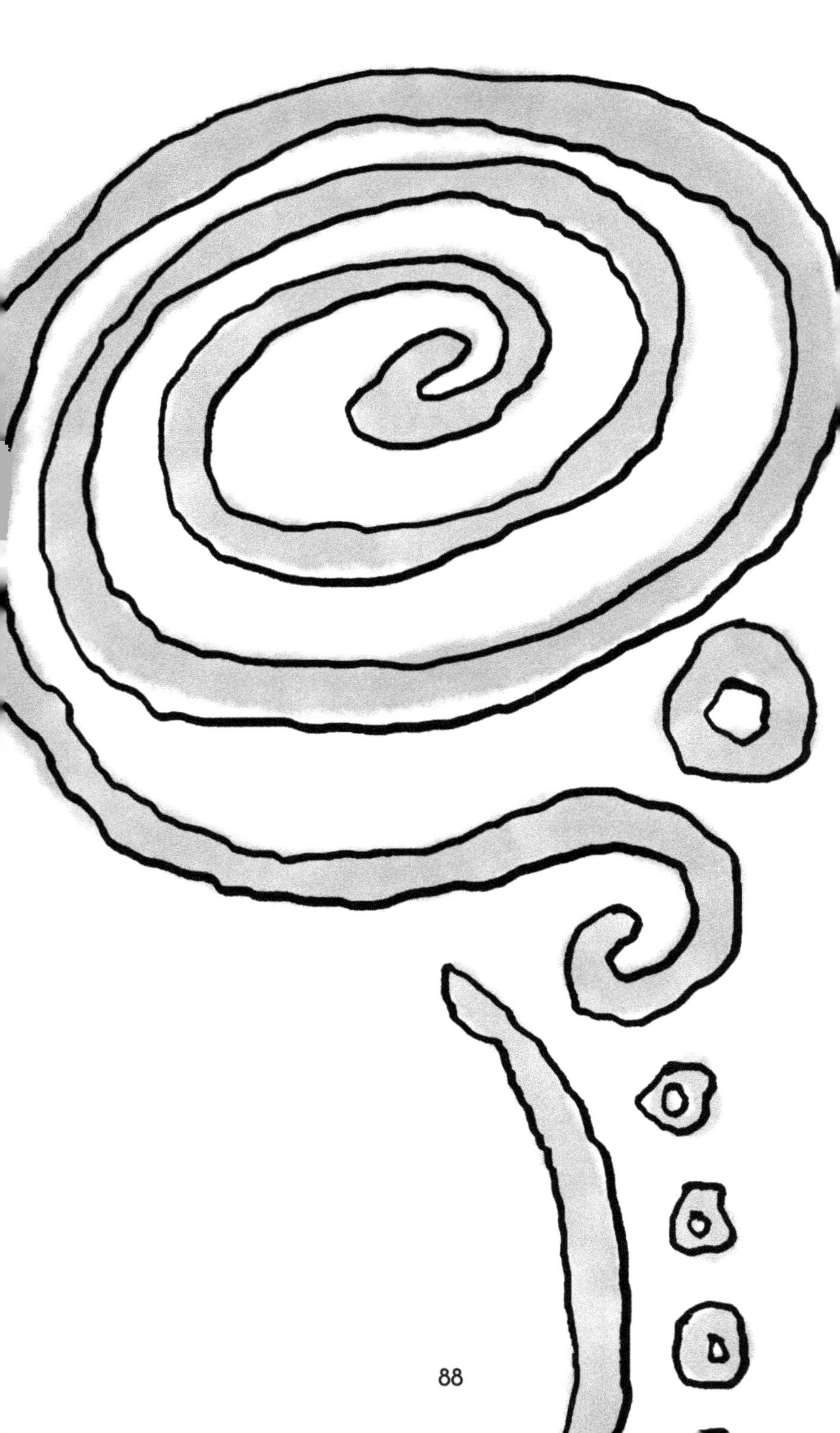

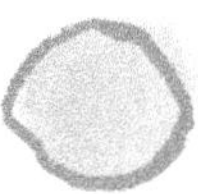

I fall to the earth

breaking amongst the hard ground

movement meeting still

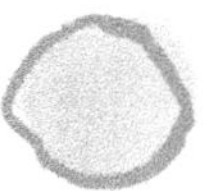

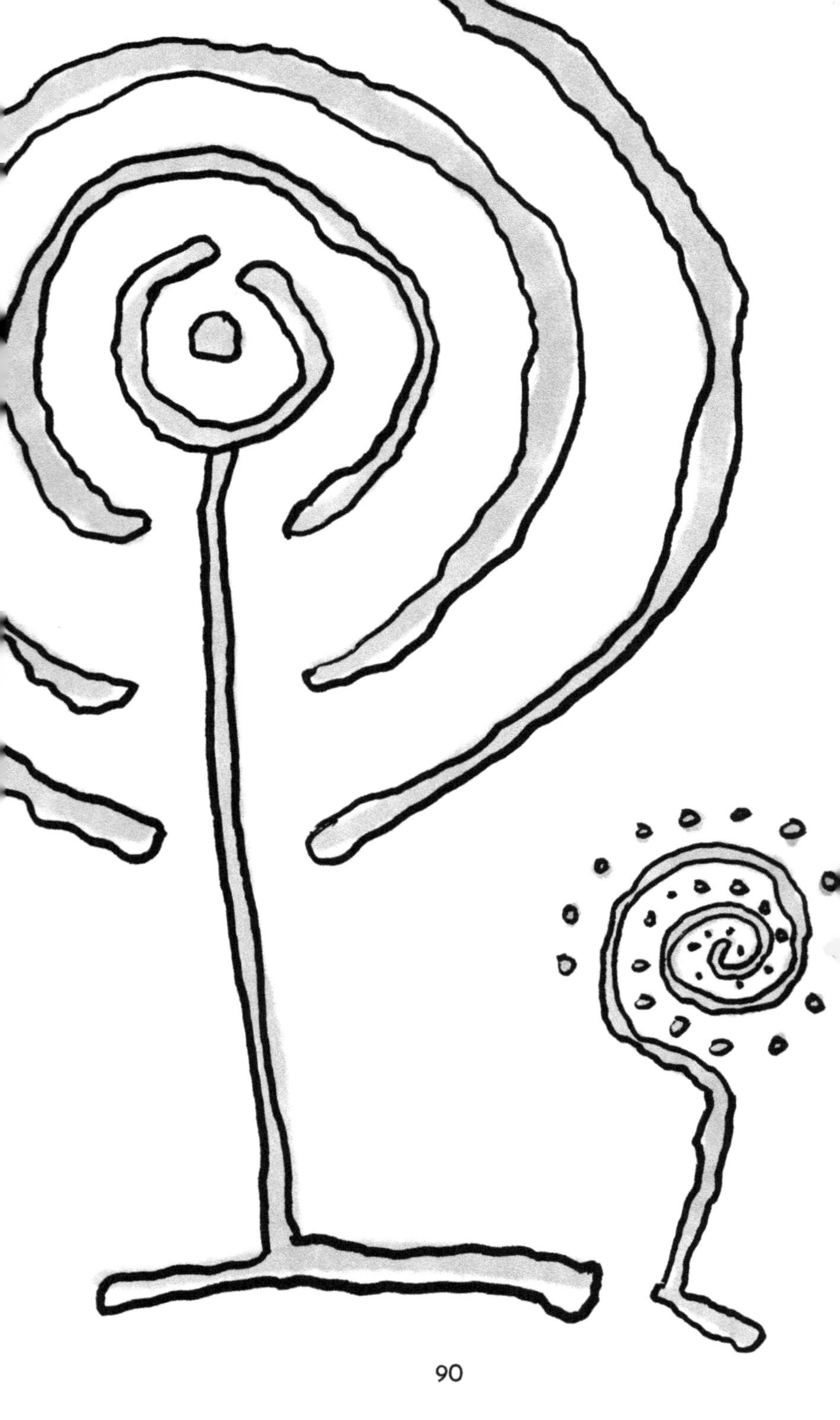

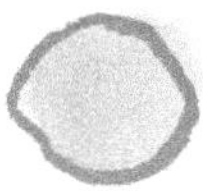

timber in the wind
shaking death rattle branches
expiration waves

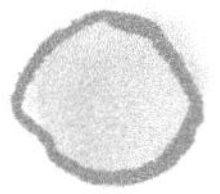

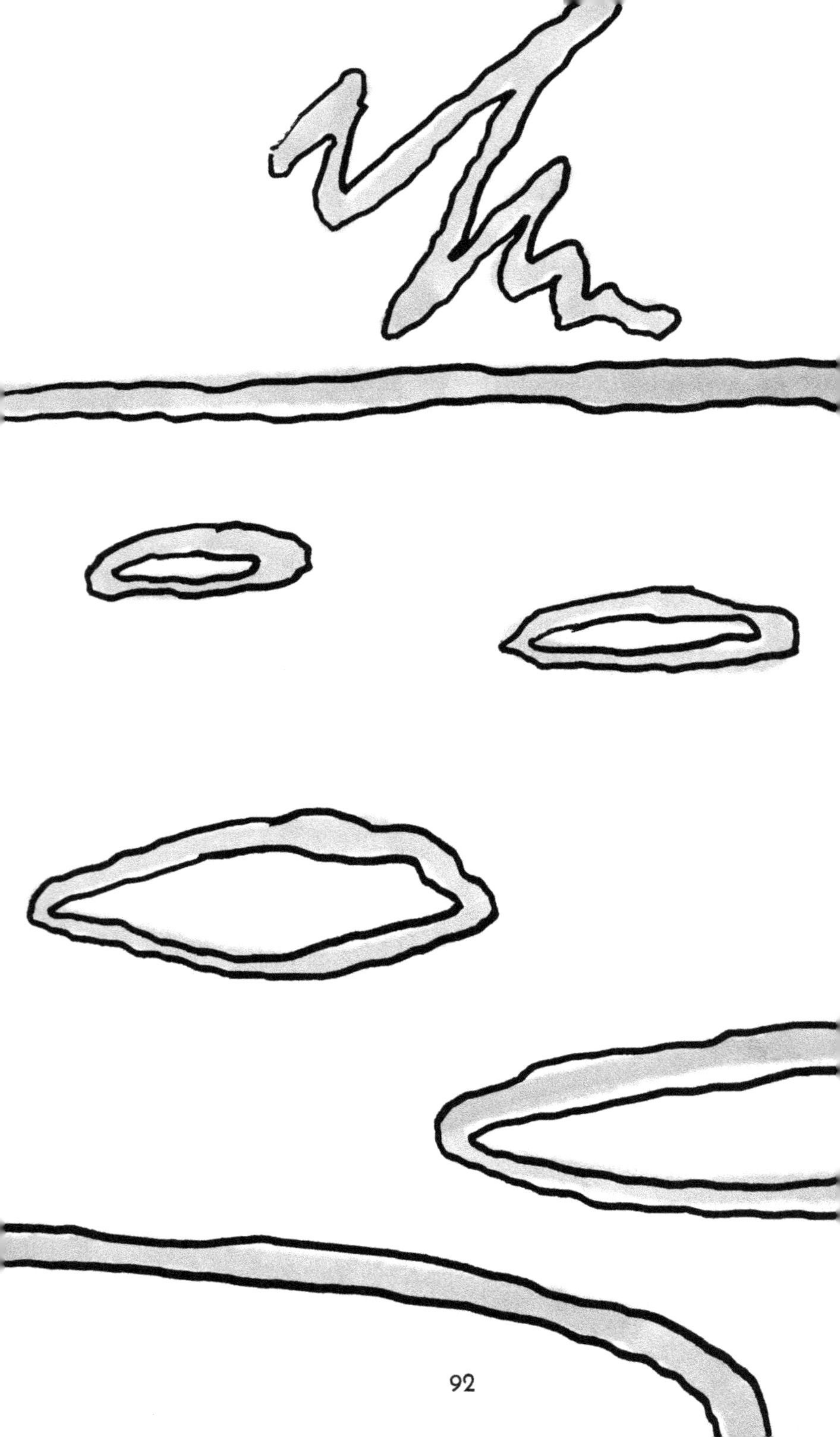

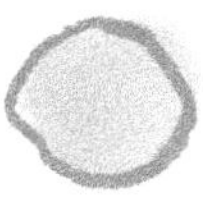

through the air it flies
horizontal momentum
retreats hastily

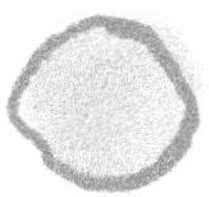

LOVE

there is a whisper
in the alchemy of our being

being apart
being together

never to know our true
independence until there is the
truth of dependence

we will always be circling around
caught in the glorious
tension

gravity of love

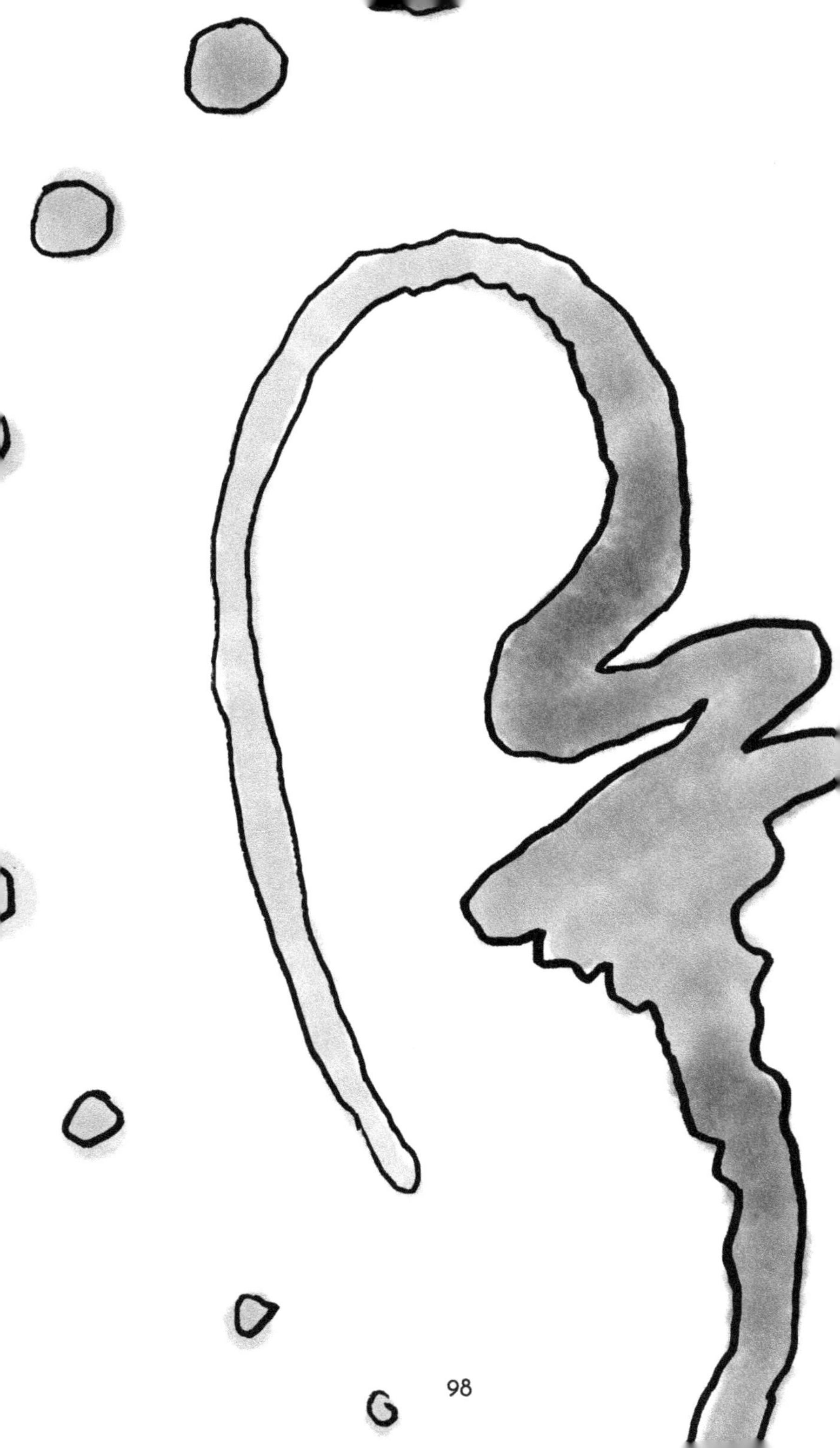

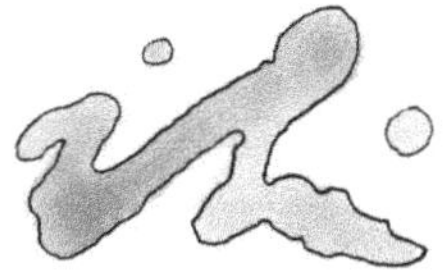

we are here today

from unexpected whispers

that bring us back home

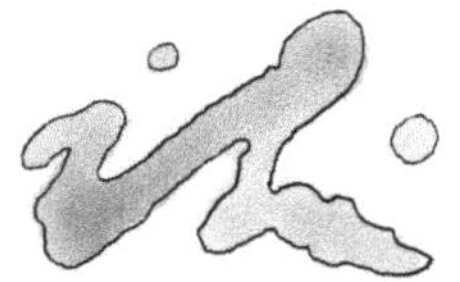

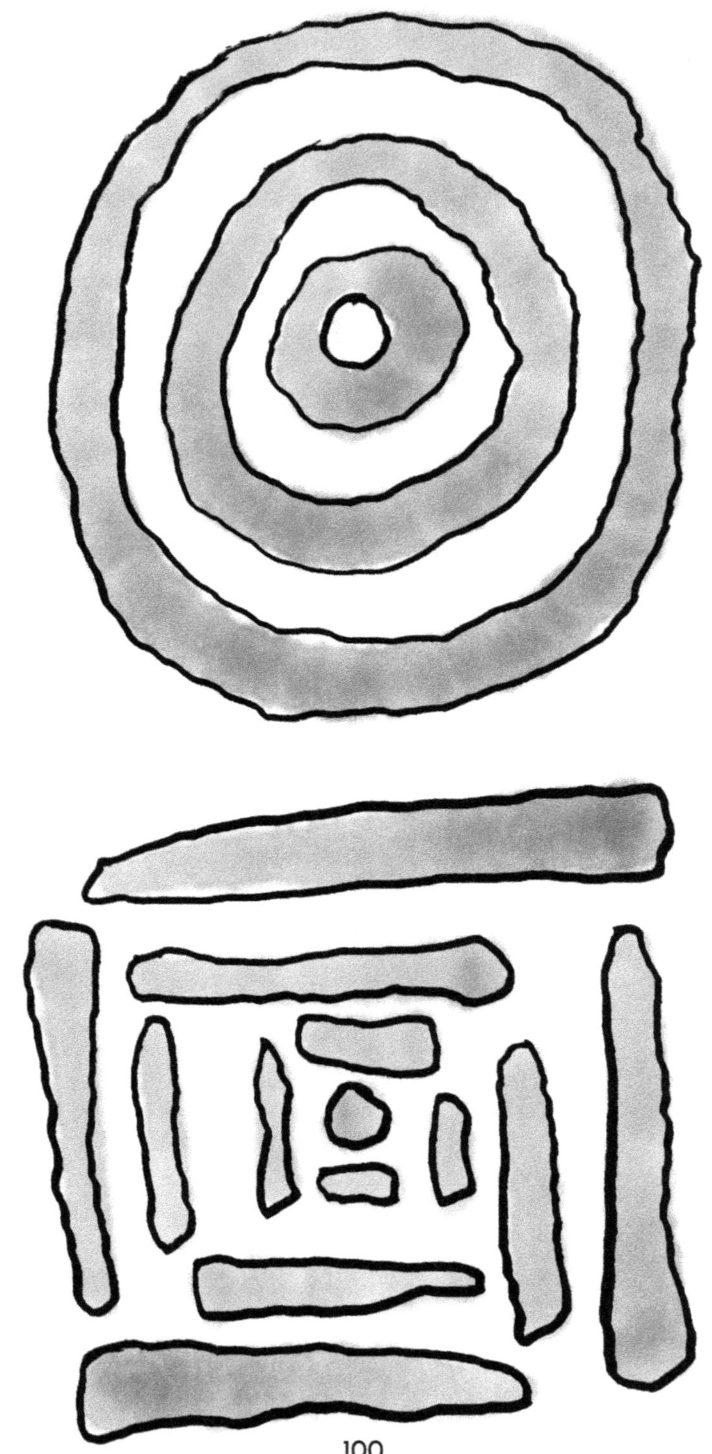

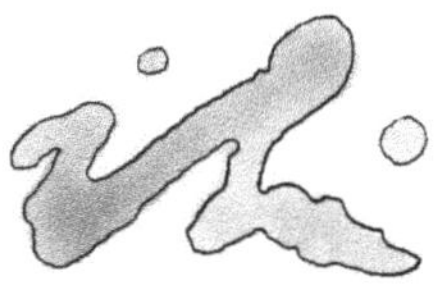

the two of a kind
are same yet so different
just puzzle pieces

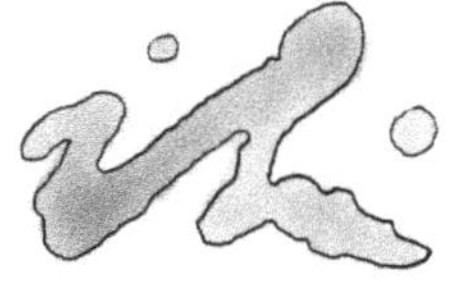

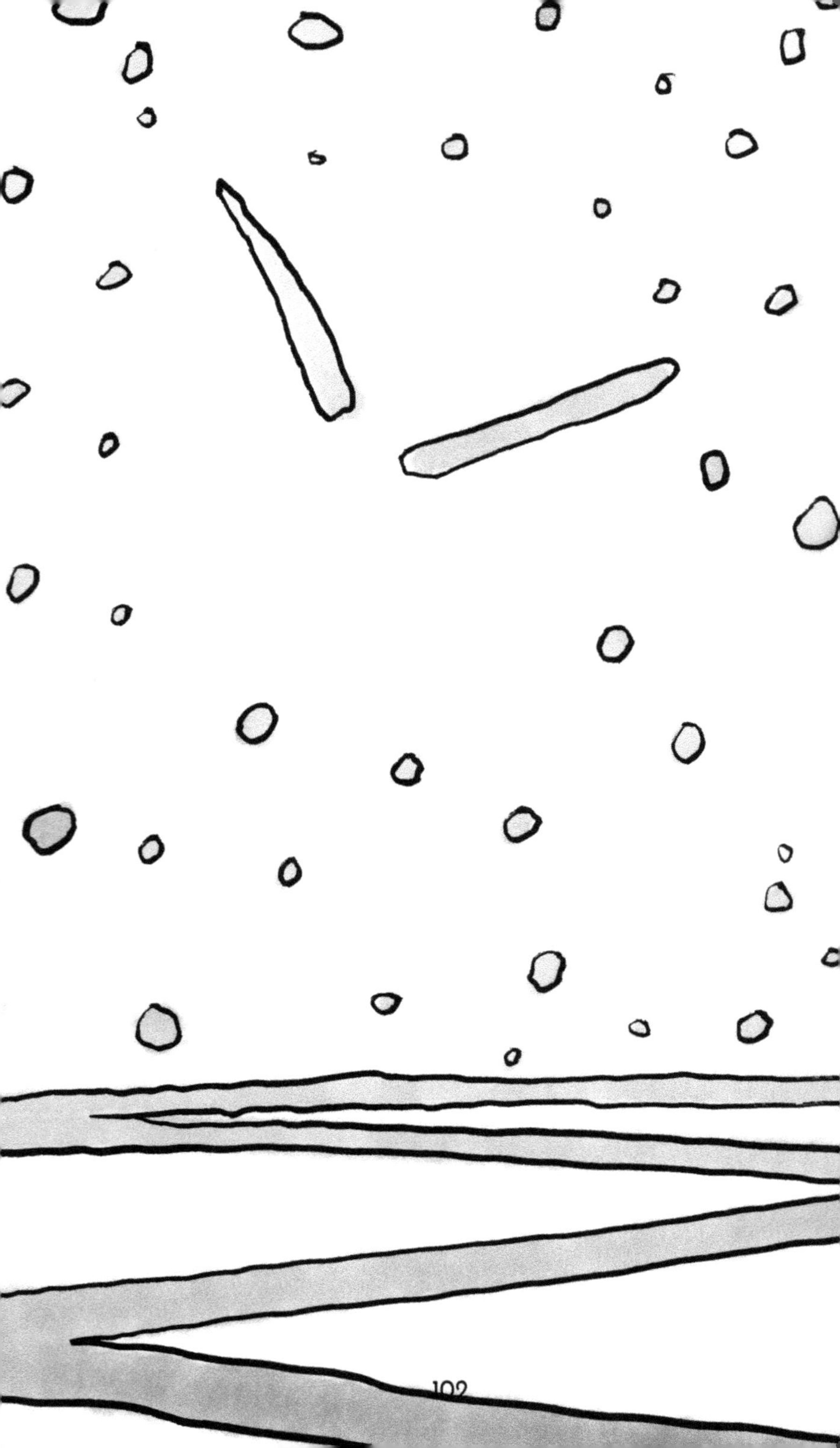

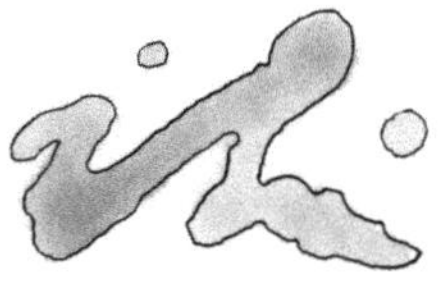

has it been ages

or just a day maybe two

there's no sense in it

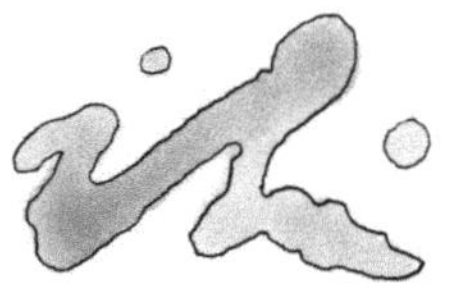

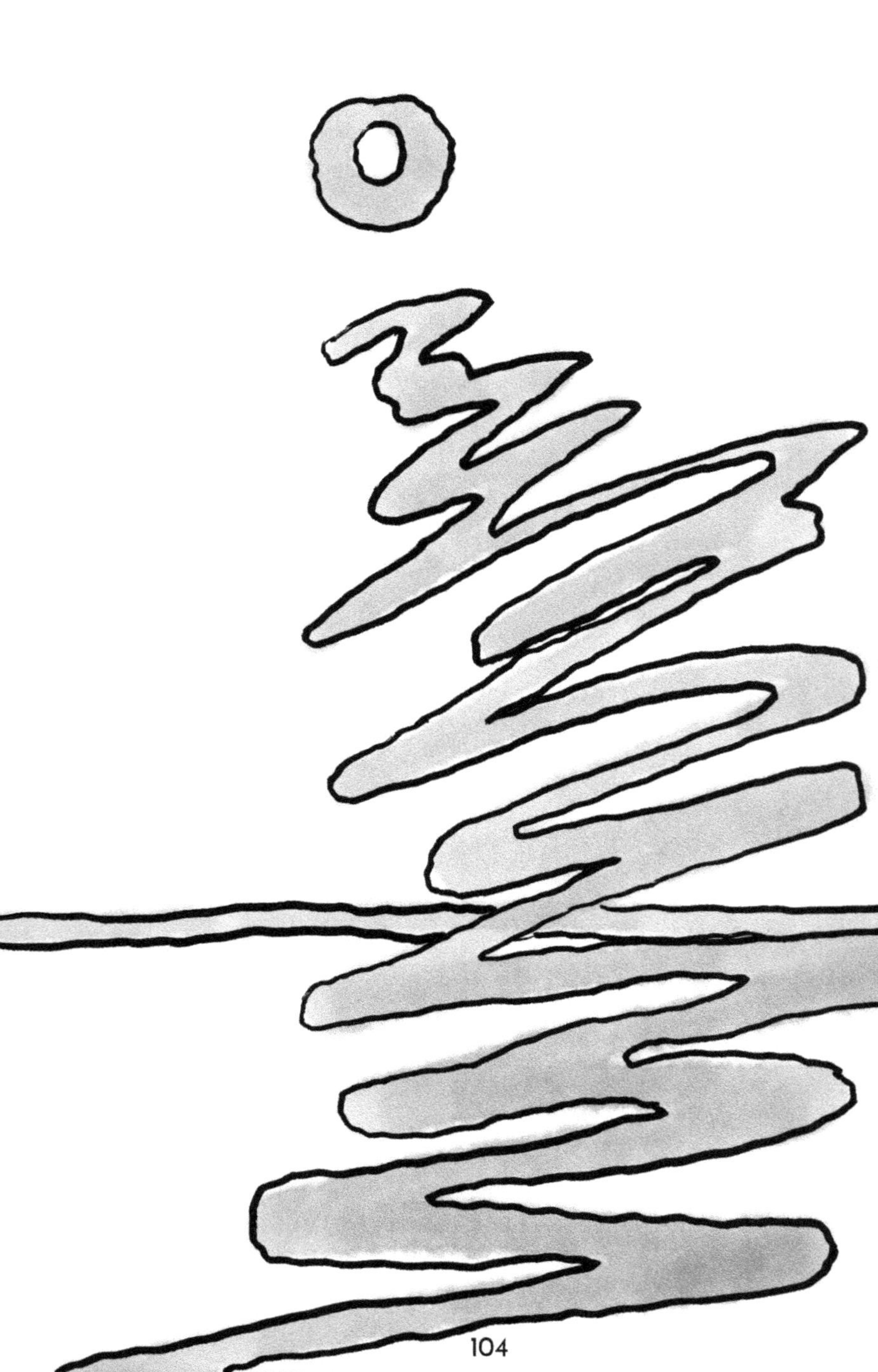

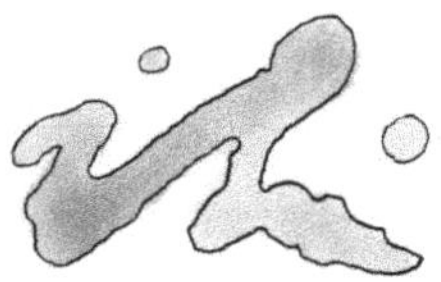

miracles of heart

create a force we don't see

the soul rising up

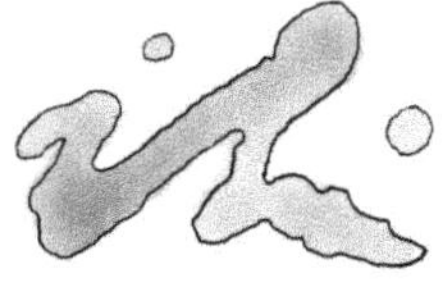

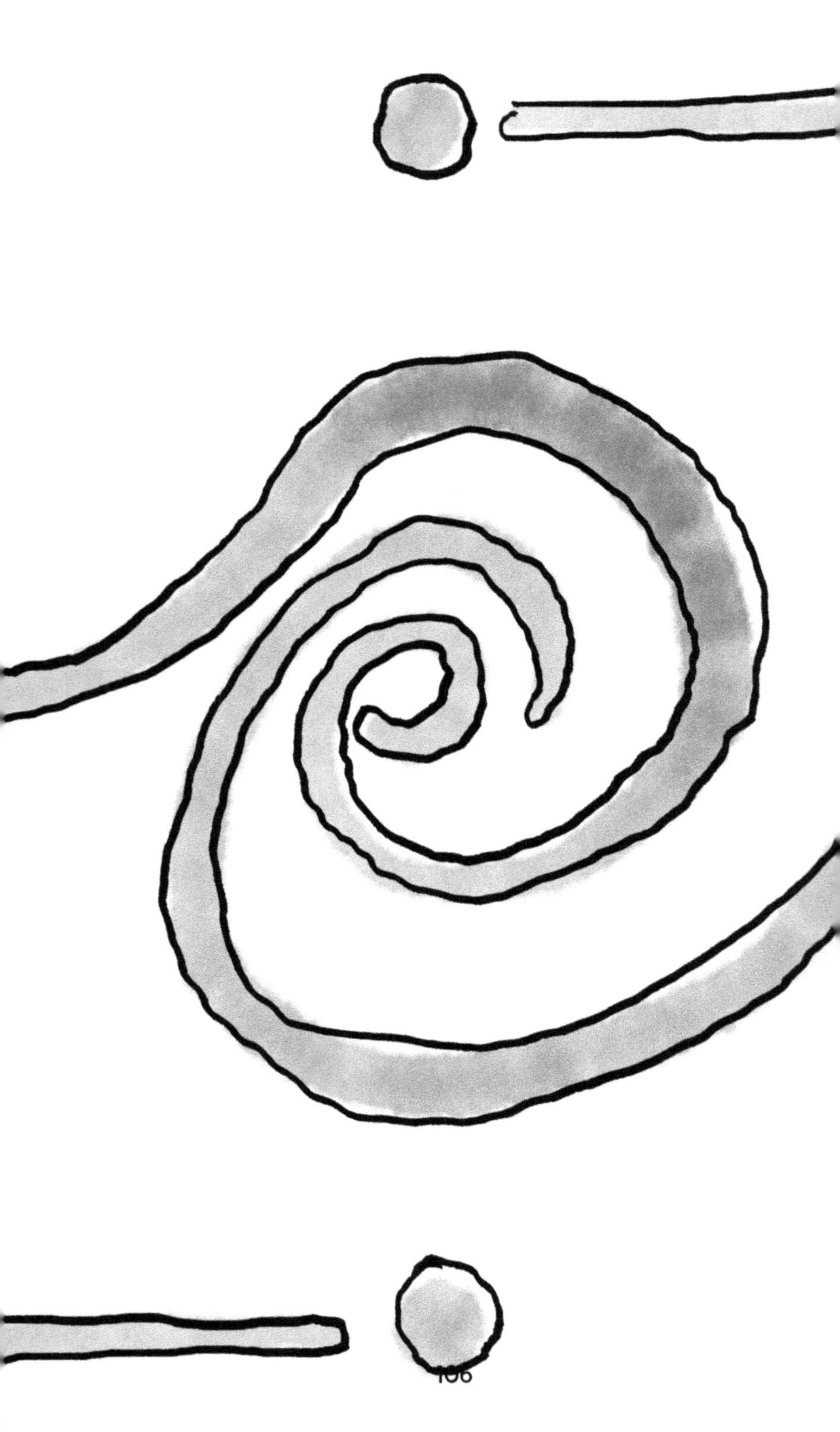

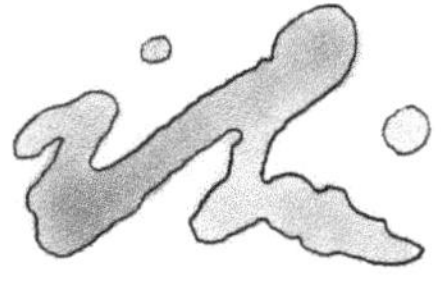

drawn together now
drawn together forever
drawn together then

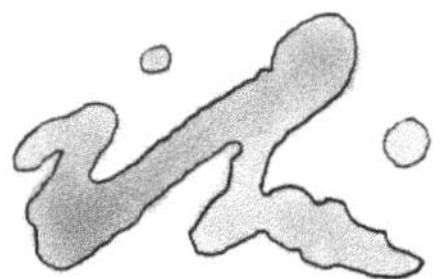

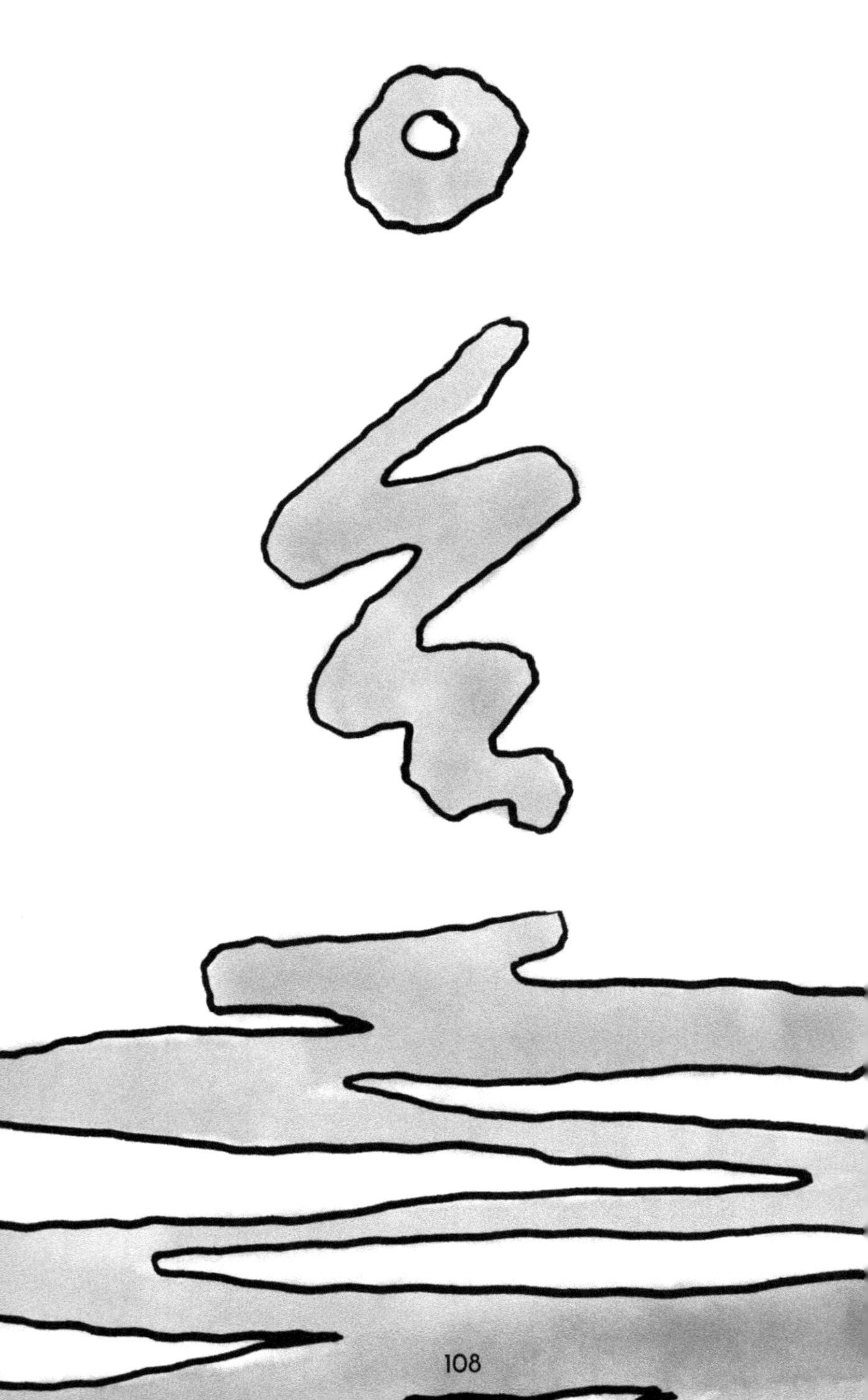

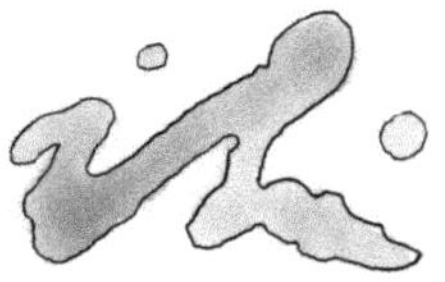

the warmth of the heart
stoked by the embers of love
wakes the soul today

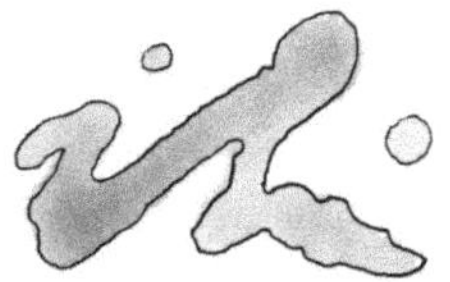

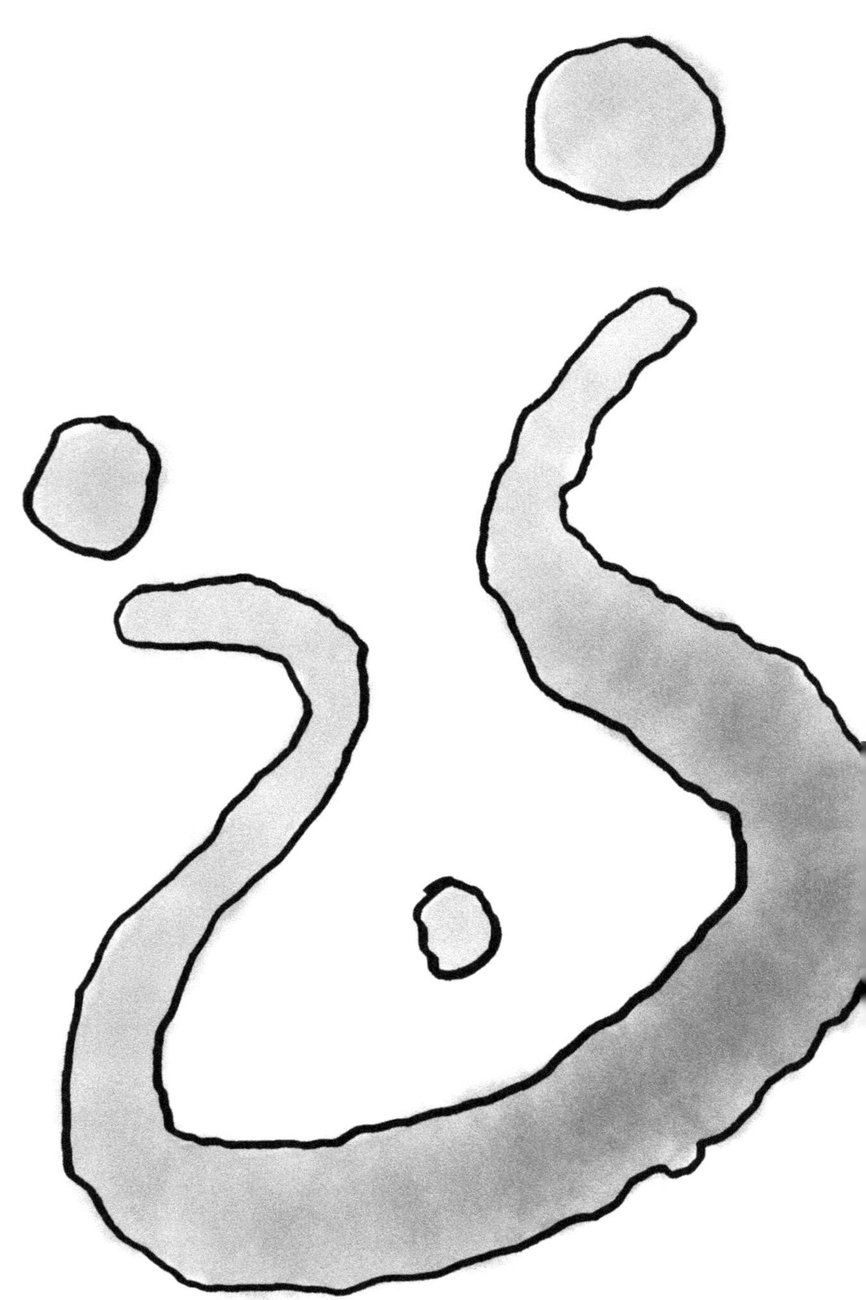

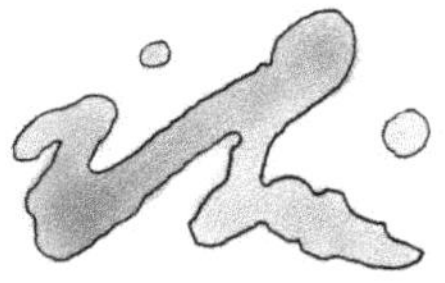

once there was but one
then there was two of a kind
become one again

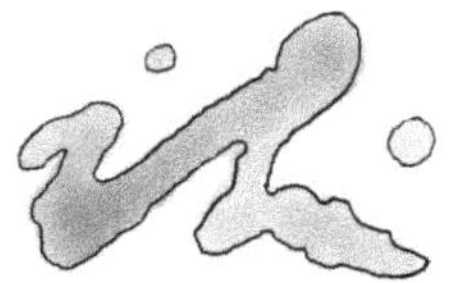

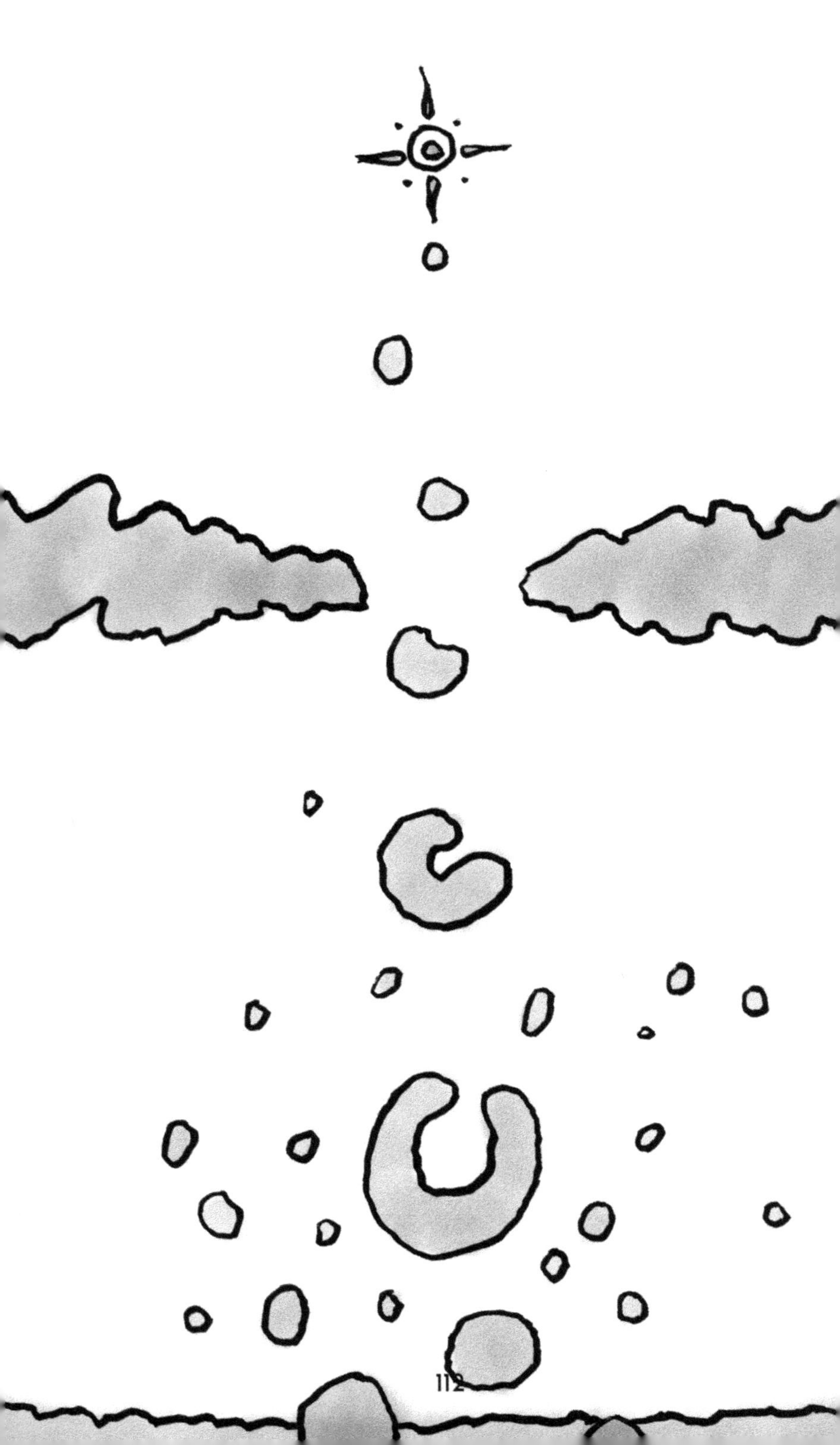

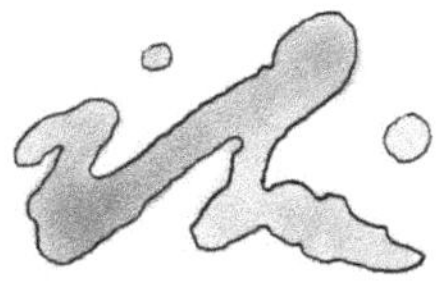

there is a purpose

we are born in this moment

to see through new eyes

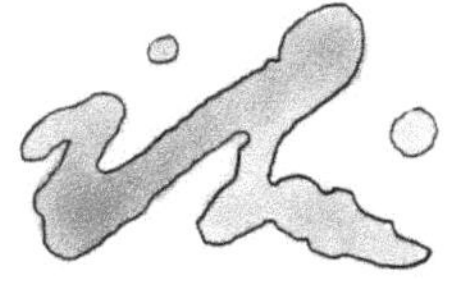

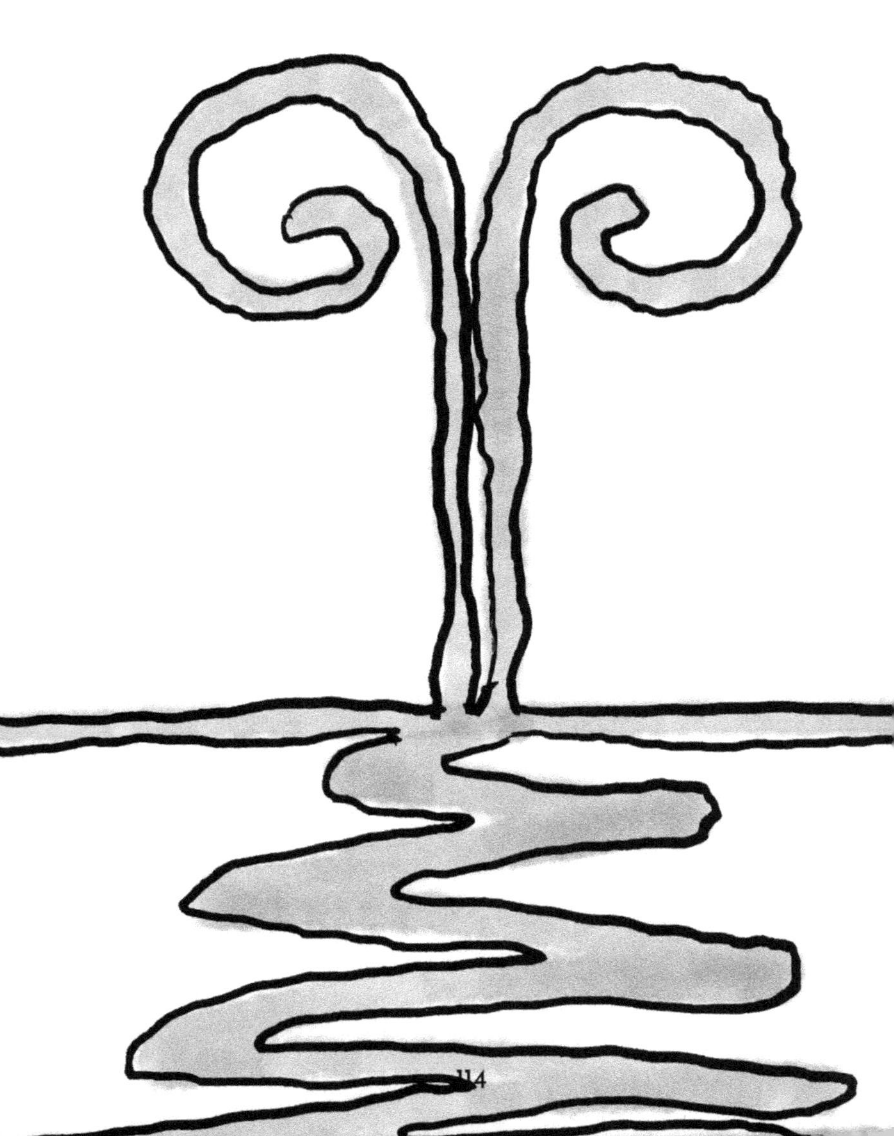

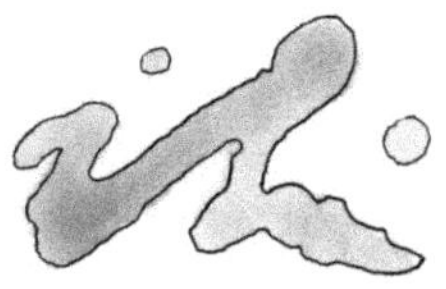

strangers we are not
never to be seen before
shadows of ourselves

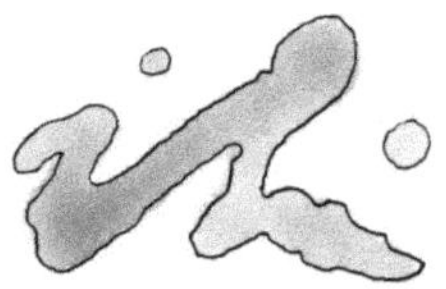

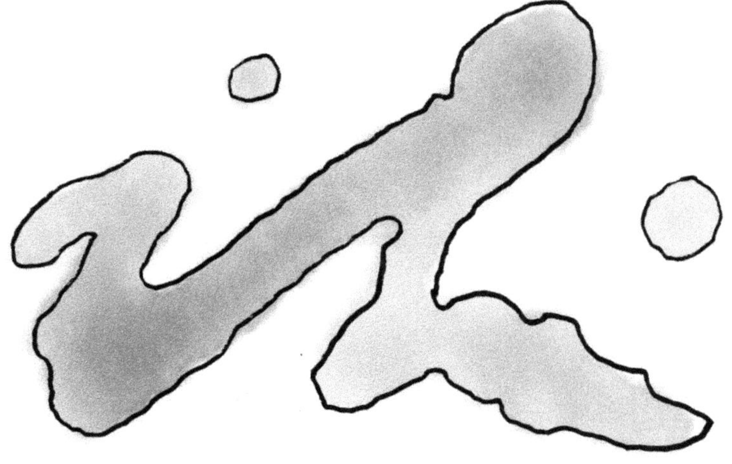

About the Author

Chuck Alen is a quasi-optimistic curmudgeon attempting to provide benefit to humanity in some modest way through random philosophizing, the written word, visual art, and sometimes even musical endeavors.

for more info:

www.chuckalen.com

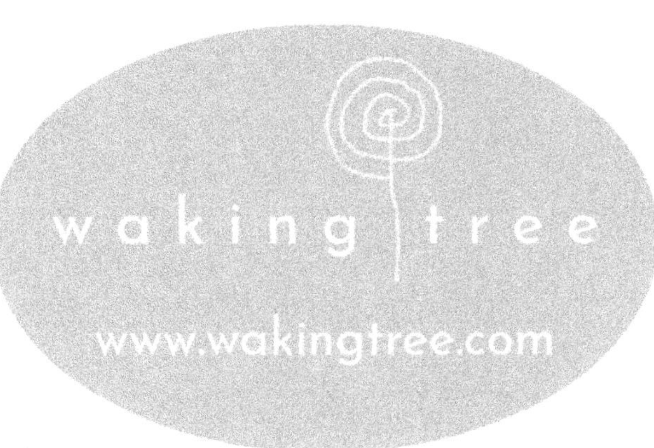
waking tree
www.wakingtree.com

www.ingramcontent.com/pod-product-compliance
Lightning Source LLC
LaVergne TN
LVHW021157160826
845679LV00024B/2146

* 9 7 9 8 9 9 3 7 3 6 6 1 7 *